M000192390

FORGOTTEN CATHOLIC HEROES

FORGOTTEN CATHOLIC HEROES

MICHAEL GENIN

Our Sunday Visitor Publishing Division
Our Sunday Visitor, Inc.
Huntington, Indiana 46750

The author and publisher are grateful to those publishers and others whose materials, whether in the public domain or protected by copyright laws, have been used in one form or another in this volume. Every reasonable effort has been made to determine copyright holders of excerpted materials and to secure permissions as necessary. If any copyrighted materials have been inadvertently used in this work without proper credit being given in one form or another, please notify Our Sunday Visitor in writing so that future printings of this work may be corrected accordingly.

Copyright © 2001 by Our Sunday Visitor Publishing Division, Our Sunday Visitor, Inc.

All rights reserved. With the exception of short excerpts for critical reviews, no part of this book may be reproduced in any manner whatsoever without permission in writing from the publisher. Write:
Our Sunday Visitor Publishing Division
Our Sunday Visitor, Inc.
200 Noll Plaza
Huntington, IN 46750

ISBN: 0-87973-516-3
LCCCN: 2001-130325

Cover design by Tyler Ottinger; photo by John Zierten
Illustrations by Tessie Bundick
Interior design by Sherri L. Hoffman

PRINTED IN THE UNITED STATES OF AMERICA

This book is dedicated to
Michael, Sarah, and Tami.
I know God loves me because
he put you into my life.

Table of Contents

꧁

The monk's assistant
hands over a large bag . . .

Introduction

The Mercedarians and Trinitarians

Imagine if you will that you are a merchant from the Mediterranean island of Sardinia. The year is 1503, some ten years after Columbus discovered the Americas, and some twenty years before the start of the Reformation.

A month ago, your tiny merchant village was raided by Algerian pirates who pillaged your community and took you and your brother prisoners. In the dark of the night you, your brother, and six villagers were herded onto a pirate galley. Once there, you were stripped naked and chained to positions at some oars. Your despair was as incredible as the stench on the ship. All around you are naked men, most of whom are sunburned, sick, and with open wounds from the lash of the whip.

The stench is unbearable. As in all galley ships, the guards refuse to unchain rowers so that they can use the bathroom. The men relieve themselves like animals in a barn. They then live in each other's squalor.

The months go by. The endless cycle of rowing, sleeping, and eating go on and on. During this time the guards have slipped a dozen or so diseased individuals overboard into the water to die.

Your galley finally arrives in Algeria. A Muslim interpreter comes on board and offers the rowers their freedom if they will convert from Christianity. The group refuses. You sit silently, resting as the pirates sell their captured treasures and restock their ship. You and your brother have a fairly certain future: you will probably die on this galley. Death by disease or drowning is your likely fate.

The boat is readying for departure when you notice a white-robed Catholic monk who is conducting a conversation with the pirate captain. The monk is a Mercedarian, a devotee of Mary, Our Lady of Mercy, Our Lady of Ransom. Your heart is full of joy at his arrival because his presence gives you hope.

The pirate, the monk, and the monk's assistant board the galley and move down to the rowers. As they near, the pirate captain pushes snuff into his nose to cover the stench. The monk's assistant hands over a large bag to the pirate. The pirate smiles greedily as he looks in the bag and pulls out a gold bracelet. He holds it up to the sun so that his fellow pirates can see the golden glare. The bag has a few more objects, mostly in the form of silver rings, necklaces, small cups, and other trinkets, all donated by European Catholics for use by the Mercedarian monks.

The pirate then turns to the monk and holds up four fingers as his other hand points to the rowers. The monk negotiates further and gets five. The monk moves down your side of the rowers and places his hand on the heads of the first five men he can reach. The men begin sobbing with joy as they are touched because they know that they are now free. The pirates are unchaining them as the monk moves forward.

You cry because you are the fifth man freed, but your brother is the sixth. He will not be freed! How will you be able to leave him? The monk is Spanish, but he can tell from your Sardinian cries and your actions that you are brothers. The monk sadly tells you in broken Sardinian that the pirates will not release any more prisoners unless they are paid today.

The monk looks at you with pity and then makes the Sign of the Cross over you. He says a prayer and then embraces you with a saintly hug. He reaches down and puts his hand on your brother's head. The pirates then unchain your brother and he is released.

You and your brother stare in shock and amazement as the monk takes off his white robe and hands it to your brother. The nearly naked monk silently takes your dear brother's place. He is chained up by the pirates as the monk's assistant guides you off the boat. You look back at the monk and see that he is preaching to the rowers and encouraging them that they are in the hands of God and that God will bless them for not converting away from the Christian faith. They are a boatload of martyrs.

You had heard of these Mercedarians and the tens of thousands of Christian slaves that they have ransomed, but you had never dreamed that they would be able to find you.

You and your brother are now free men, having been granted passage to Spain. The Mercedarians there are gathering money from their monasteries to ransom more prisoners and provide transportation for them to get back to their homes.

The decades pass and in the year 1540 you are on a merchant trip to Holland with your brother. A merchant approaches you and tries to convert you with tales of the evil and corruption of the Catholic Spanish monarchs and the Catholic Church. He then shows you selected Bible phrases from the Book of Revelation as proof that the world will end in the next ten years. He also offers biblical proof that the Church of Rome is corrupt. He urges you to convert.

You and your brother respond by showing him swaths of wool that you have cut from the Mercedarian monk's white robe and attached to a chord around your necks. You tell the merchant your story and ask him, "How can an evil and corrupt Church produce thousands of saintly men such as these?" The merchant has no response.

The Mercedarians

It is interesting to note that the Mercedarians are often overlooked in histories written by those wishing to condemn the Catholic Church during the pre-Reformation years. The Order of Our Lady of Mercy, Our Lady of Ransom (more popularly known as the Mercedarians), was founded in Spain in the year 1218 by a group of crusading knights who had decided to become monks.

The goal of the Mercedarians was to ransom Christians who had been taken captive by barbarians or Muslims. This was a much-needed function, since prisoners of raids or wars were made slaves unless they were ransomed or converted to Islam. The slaves could be thrown into the galleys, harems, or lead mines or be disposed of as their masters saw fit.

By the 1300s the founding knights had moved on, and the Mercedarians became a strictly religious entity with the members taking the common vows of poverty, chastity, and obedience. They also took a fourth vow, the vow being that they would take a Christian slave's place if they could not provide enough ransom money to free them.

The Mercedarians and their contributing affiliates (the Trinitarians) operated about eight hundred monasteries throughout Europe. They were successful in providing ransoms for approximately one million Christians who had been captured by the barbarian tribes of Europe and the Islamic peoples of Africa and the Middle East.

Their activities, though, have gone largely unnoticed by modern scholars. *The Dictionary of Saints* by John J. Delaney (Doubleday, 1980) has been enlisted to give us an idea of the activities of various Mercedarians:

Blessed Serapion — He was an English soldier who became a Mercedarian. He went to Algiers to secure the release of Christian prisoners of the Moors, a Muslim people. He was held hostage at Algiers for the balance of ransom that he was to pay for a group of prisoners. Serapion was crucified in the year 1240 by his captors when it was discovered that while in prison he had converted several Islamites to Christianity.

Blessed Peter Armengol — This Mercedarian, whose date of birth is usually given as the year 1238, made two trips to ransom Christian captives of the Moors. On the second trip he gave himself as hostage when he did not have money to free eighteen young boys. Peter was hanged when the promised payment did not arrive on time. When he was cut down he was found to be still alive. He died ten days later due to his sufferings. According to some sources, he probably died in 1304.

St. Peter Nolasco — Born around the year 1189, he was a Spaniard who inherited a fortune at age fifteen. He used his wealth to ransom Christian prisoners of the Moors. He and St. Raymond Peñafort are credited with founding the Mercedarians. St. Peter was imprisoned several times as a hostage for Christian prisoners.

The Order of Our Lady of Mercy was just one of the many noble religious orders that flourished during the time of the Reformation. The Mercedarians were joined by the

Trinitarians, also known as the Order of the Most Holy Trinity. The Trinitarians were formed in 1240 by St. Felix of Valois and St. John of Matha. Their goal was to ransom captives from the Moors. The order soon had six hundred monasteries spread throughout France, Spain, Italy, and England. One third of the monastery revenues went to ransoming captives. The monks of these orders operated in North Africa.

One would be hard-pressed to find a more noble and selfless group of Christians in any time period before or since their foundation.

The Reason for This Book

A few years ago Pope John Paul II announced that he was "asking forgiveness" for past sins and injustices that had been committed by individuals working in the name of the Catholic Church. He also in turn offered an unconditional forgiveness to those who in the past had committed sins against Catholics. I remember reading a synopsis of the proclamation and thinking how profound it was. I, like many others, began hoping that it would have a healing effect that would help unite Christians, Jews, Muslims, and those of other faiths.

To my surprise, I began reading newspaper "letters to the editors" in which people were stating that Catholics had a lot to ask forgiveness for but basically had never had anyone persecute them since the time of the Roman Empire. The tone was that, until the recent past, Catholics were almost generally corrupt and could not care less about the teachings of Christ.

It is my sincere belief that the exact opposite is true. Throughout the Church's history, Catholics have given up everything they had to follow Jesus and carry out his commands. I believe that there have been good and bad Catholics, just as there have been good and bad Protestants, Muslims, and Jews. There are, though, literally hundreds of thousands of Catholic heroes whose efforts have been forgotten by modern Western culture. This book has been written so that their dedication and love for Christ and his Church shall remain forgotten no more.

I would like to add that, although the stories are based on the lives of saintly men and women, many of our heroes and heroines in this work are composites of these holy individuals. I have taken the liberty of expanding on them in an effort to make a point, to describe an event with force and vigor so as to bring out both the good and bad of human nature, and to make other alterations for similar considerations. An example of the latter is the use of both real and fictitious names, such as Janissary (real) and Gbur (fictitious), in Chapter 5. I hope you will indulge me in this, keeping in mind that my main reason for doing this is to ensure that the memory of our forgotten Catholic heroes remains alive and well. ✝

The ten-year-old girl wonders whether Katrina
has swallowed pebbles or grapes . . .

CHAPTER ONE

The Servants of the Sick

Imagine that it is the middle of the fourteenth century. About sixty years before Joan of Arc is born in France. A ten-year-old girl living near the Convent of St. Columba in northwest Bavaria is standing by her village well. Four days earlier the people of the village waited in vain for the Sisters of St. Columba. The nuns were scheduled to act out a play detailing the life of Christ. The sisters never arrived. There was no explanation given for their failure to show up as expected.

The girl wonders how they are doing and why none of the two hundred some nuns at the convent have made their biweekly visit to the village. They usually come here to purchase linens and supplies. They also used to come on Sundays to teach Bible stories and religion. The nuns, however, are nowhere to be found.

It is morning and the young girl's frail ten-year-old frame has just hoisted a bucket of water from the village well. She is distracted from her duties when she hears a pounding of hooves down the trail to the convent. The girl looks down the valley and notices a young novice nun riding a horse as fast as she can. It is apparent from the novice's actions that she has never ridden before. The poor nun is trying to ride sidesaddle at a gallop. She bounces around in the saddle like a doll being tossed by a playful puppy. With each bump she becomes airborne for a second and then crashes back into the saddle. She is holding on for dear life. The nun draws nearer and is recognized as Katrina, a fourteen-year-old Swabian girl who is preparing to take the vows of poverty, chastity, and obedience. The ten-year-old is not only shocked at Katrina's poor riding ability but just the fact that she is riding at all. It is à rare sight to see a young peasant girl riding a horse, horses being generally reserved for merchants and nobles.

Katrina's horse pounds through the village and heads for the fork in the road. She says nothing; the horse hesitates and half-slides in the muddy road. It steadies itself and hurtles down the left fork. The ten-year-old wonders to herself whether the horse or the rider chose the route that was taken. She watches in amazement as Katrina protests the horse's choice and vainly tries to manhandle it back to the right. Katrina fails and the animal continues left as Katrina tumbles down into the mud. The horse gallops some forty yards before it slows and turns to see what has happened. The horse, a bit hesitant, finally stops. It chooses to casually graze by the roadside, having partially dislodged its bit and bridle as Katrina fell.

By now Katrina has sat up in the mud and loosened her collar as she stares blankly off into the distance. She is barefoot and begins to mumble something in an incoherent voice. Fortunately, the ten-year-old girl is in possession of a full bucket of water. She puts the wooden bucket in her right hand and, leaning her body to the left, she makes her way to Katrina.

Katrina is a pitiful sight, apparently out of her mind with fever. The ten-year-old stands directly in front of the nun, perhaps a foot away, but Katrina doesn't realize she is there. Her glazed eyes cannot perceive the ten-year-old's presence.

"Kat! Kat!" the girl calls but receives no response. She reaches down to touch Katrina's face. "Katrina!" she yells as she pokes Katrina's cheek. Katrina's skin feels as hot as a skillet: a sad combination of 106-degree fever and the modest but heavy nun's robes that Katrina is wearing.

"Water!" Katrina gasps as the ten-year-old's touch brings her out of her stupor. The child pours water on Katrina's forehead and then hands her the bucket to drink. Katrina takes it feebly but purposely from her hands. Her lips touch the uptilted bucket's wooden rim and the water dribbles into her mouth.

When she has had her fill she pushes the bucket away weakly and mutters, "Thank God!" The ten-year-old looks at her as Katrina absentmindedly pulls her collar to let out the heat that is welling up beneath her robes. Katrina is exhausted. She was once a beautiful girl. She looks pitiful now, her tongue being covered with a white mucus and both her hands pushing onto the base of her arched back. Katrina grimaces from the severe back pains that have racked her for days.

The ten-year-old notices that Katrina's neck looks like she has swallowed round pebbles or whole grapes that have stuck just under her skin. Her lymph nodes are swollen with disease. Her skin is blotchy with blood-red marks that look like bruises that have not had time to turn black. A few of them are dark and turning the color of coal.

"What could be wrong with her?" the ten-year-old thinks to herself as she raises the bucket to her lips to drink her fill.

Katrina rests for a few minutes and then feebly asks the girl to fetch her horse. "I have a message . . . an urgent message for the abbot of Beyersdorf," she says in a raspy voice as she looks down at the ground, and her callused hands return to her arching back. The girl helps Katrina out of the mud and then retrieves her horse. Within a half-hour Katrina is ready to go.

"If you want the horse to go right, pull its right ear hard!" the ten-year-old girl advises, although she herself has never ridden a horse. Katrina, smiling wanly, tries to put on a brave face. It is apparent that she is terrified of the beast that she now must ride. Undaunted, she pulls up the rosary beads that are tied to her waist. She stares at the figure of Jesus crucified on the cross. Katrina mutters something to herself and then closes her eyes briefly. She then looks up, grabs the reins, and tries to mount. She fails, being too weak to climb on. At this point the girl steps forward and lets Katrina use her hands as a stirrup. Katrina finally manages to get on the horse and trots off sidesaddle. The young girl returns to the town well, refills her bucket, and walks back to her hut.

Two days pass with little activity in the village. Nothing has been heard from the convent. The villagers are worried as they notice several of the convent's sheep wandering between the wooden huts, feeding on clumps of grass and stray pieces of grain. The men of the village are concerned for the nuns at the convent.

"Bandits! . . . or worse!" they murmur among themselves as several of them gather staves and rakes, ready to protect their village. They discuss plans to send a few "scouts" down to see how the nuns are doing. That is when the young girl tells them the story about Katrina's ride. The men quickly lose heart. They will readily die to defend their families from brigands, but resistance to evil like that is futile. The men feel defenseless and mill about aimlessly until they see help coming up the road.

Help is in the form of forty monks and a wagon from the Abbey of Beyersdorf. From a distance the men look like bearded dwarves from an ancient fairy tale. They seem so small compared to the huge Clydesdale that is pulling their wagon. The young girl marvels at the size of the beast. She has never seen anything so big. It is fairly early in the morning and steam is billowing out of the horse's nostrils as his moist breath mixes with the chilly air. To the child's eye it is like smoke from a fire-breathing dragon that is working up a flame.

The monks pause but a moment to ask for directions to the convent. The villagers warn them of the strange events, but the monks do not appear to be afraid. They are grim but determined.

"Katrina has told us," one of the monks states as he points to the back of the wagon. There Katrina lies sleeping, next to two monks who have just this morning shown signs of the illness. The red blotches on Katrina's skin are now oil-black as the disease has progressed to its final stages. Small trickles of dried blood mar the corners of her mouth and her right hand. "The devil is with us," the monk says as he grimly states the obvious.

Mothers start shooing their children into their wooden huts. Other parents help the monks fill their water flasks from the town well. Some do it out of Christian charity, others to hurry the monks out of town (and to take the sickness with them). "We wanted Katrina to stay at the abbey, but she insisted on returning to her convent," the monk comments as he shakes his head sadly. "I fear that she has not much time left with us."

The young girl watches as the monks disappear down the road to the convent. It will be a sad week for her. As the days go by, one person after another falls victim to disease. The monks now come through the village every morning to collect the sick and bring them to the convent for care and prayer. As they make their rounds, the ten-year-old calls for them to take her ailing father and mother. Earlier, the girl had noticed their fever, their white tongues, the red blotches, and the swollen bumps. She knows what comes next.

Her parents refuse to leave her by herself. They fear that the village's entire population might soon be gone. Almost two thirds of the villagers are either dead or dying of the mysterious disease. The monks, though, have no problem with the girl remaining at her parents' side.

"She can help tend them," the monk says as he lifts her into the wagon. When he does this, her cheek touches his skin. He is burning up with fever too, yet he still wears the wool habit that almost entirely covers his body. His tongue is white, but he has no blotches on his skin.

"How can this be?" the girl's ten-year-old mind wonders as the cart takes her down the road. "They always get blotches." Her mind soon returns to her sick parents. She wonders what would happen to them — and her — if the monks and nuns were not here to provide for the villagers' care.

One hour and three miles later she enters the convent. It has changed dramatically in the past two months. Most of the two hundred nuns are now sick, dead, or dying. The hospital at the convent is manned by only thirty nuns and about fifteen monks. The convent hospital's eighty straw beds are filled to capacity. Some beds hold two, some hold three, but all the victims manage as best they can. Other patients lie in piles of straw on the floor. The place is lit by hundreds of candles with a few stained-glass windows providing light from above. Nuns and monks are scurrying tirelessly about the room. Some carry water, some carry soup. Others turn straw-mattress bags. About a dozen pray with people as they pass from this world to the next. The ten-year-old girl is healthy, so nobody pays much attention to her. She can move freely and come and go as she pleases.

The girl witnesses the sad sight of a nun holding the hand of a dying person as they pray. The ten-year-old moves on and sees her Aunt Teresa lying in a bed with two other ladies. A nun holds one hand while the lady lying beside her holds the other. They are all saying the Rosary as they prepare for eternity. A priest has been working his way from bed to bed hearing confessions, providing Communion, and giving the Last Rites (as the sacrament of the anointing of the sick used to be called). Other monks are occasionally moving bodies to the courtyard for burial.

"Sister! Sister Agatha!" the ten-year-old calls to a nun standing nearby. She is positioned slightly behind the nun but still recognizes her from the market. She yells louder, but the nun does not respond. "Sister Agatha!" she yells as she moves around to where the nun can see her. The nun finally sees her. She smiles and gives the girl a hug as she reaches to pick her up. The nun's back is bothering her, so she cannot complete her task. "Where is my mother?" she asks the nun.

Sister Agatha shakes her head negatively and points at her own ears. She yells, "I cannot hear anymore! Not since yesterday!" The girl notices that she too has the disease. The nun smiles stoically just the same.

The little girl wanders around a bit and notices Katrina working out in the courtyard. Kat is using a hand ax to chop wood for the fire. She is struggling quite a bit, but she is apparently on the mend. The girl had thought for certain that Kat was done for, at least in this world. Kat puts down the ax and finds it easier to break the sticks by standing them on end and leaning into them. Soon she has enough wood to carry into the convent kitchen for the fire. It is only forty yards, but she must stop three times to catch her breath. She is exhausted and deserves bed rest. But she carries on.

This macabre scene goes on for three days. Most of the remaining nuns and monks are sick and exhausted, but they struggle on. Almost everyone from the village is either dead or being cared for at the convent. The elder monks and nuns have been buried, and now, due to attrition, the mother superior is a twenty-two-year-old who has been at the convent for just three years. She is calling out the window for Katrina but calling her by the name Mary Catherine.

"Here, Sister!" Kat says as she puts down the vegetables she was preparing and struggles to the hall. Kat is fourteen and walking with a cane. She is looking better though. The color is back in her skin, but her strength is gone. Not only is she exhausted, both mentally and physically, but her body, joints, and immune system have been totally devastated. She starts to faint but catches herself and moves on.

The ten-year-old watches as the new mother superior asks Kat if she knows how to read either German or Latin. The nuns are trying to read the Gospel to the bedridden victims. They are stymied by the fact that the older nuns and monks are either dead or too sick to be of help. Kat apologizes that she has not had time to learn to read. She wonders if Sister Clare might be able to read from her sickbed. It is no use. Sister Clare's vision had been blurred even before the epidemic had started.

Another day passes and now the Sisters are desperate. Victims from other villages have arrived. There are about two hundred patients in the convent plus about fifty orphans living in the barn with what is left of the cattle. The livestock are almost gone and there is little food available. The carts keep arriving and there are now almost three hundred victims at the convent. There are only seven healthy nuns and six monks. The monks spend most of their time digging graves and physically moving people about the building. One monk must devote his entire day to making candles so that the caregivers can see at night. One nun spends all her time hauling water to the convent. Another chops wood while two others prepare food. That leaves three nuns to provide twenty-four-hour care to the living. The entire staff is constantly praying.

Mother Superior decides that something needs to change or all the sick will die of neglect. There are about fifteen healthy villagers at the convent, but they spend their time caring for the orphans and watching the livestock. Few have the courage to face the plague like the monks and nuns.

"Kat!" the new mother superior calls, forgetting Kat's new name at the convent. They huddle for a bit, looking so old standing next to each other. Both have been deathly sick. "Can you take the orphans on the road to the bishop of Munchen?"

"I think so," Kat replies with a look of concern on her face.

"Take whatever valuables you can find to pay for their care."

"Yes, Mother!" Kat says, curtsying shakily with one hand on her cane. She heads to the chapel, where she gathers up a few gold and silver candlesticks and wraps them in some fine religious linens.

"We must go now," she says as she gently puts her callused hands behind the ten-year-old's neck and guides her along. The girl does not mind leaving the convent, since both her parents are gone. Kat leads her to the courtyard, where they gather the orphans who are waiting in the barn. A few villagers assist as the orphans file by the well and through the kitchen. Everyone gets a drink and grabs as many raw vegetables as each one of them can carry. Soon the group is on the road to the village.

The village has changed dramatically. In just the short time that the epidemic has started, the abandoned community has fallen into disrepair. The orphans stop at the well and drink their fill. No one dares enter the huts, as they have only the memory of death.

The spirit of death, however, is broken by the sound of singing coming up the road. It is the joyful sound of nuns praying the Rosary in Latin. The prayer sounds both holy and powerful at the same time. The voices grow louder. Soon the first few nuns come into sight. The crowd of refugee children becomes ecstatic at the sight of about fifty nuns and three wagons. The bishop of Munchen has sent them to join the fight.

The children, although fairly certain that they have been rescued, still have some doubts. Yet it is undeniable that the orphans, Kat, the village, and the convent will never be the same.

The Black Death and Its Effect on the European Catholic Church

During the fourteenth century, most of Europe was ravaged by the bubonic plague, which was better known as the Black Death. It spread quickly, with victims usually living less than a week before they expired. Modern scholars estimate that there were almost a hundred million people in Europe before the start of the Black Death. Within a few years of the dreaded disease's onset, only seventy-five million people were left. Many of the survivors were physically and mentally ravaged. The Black Death died down at times but flared up at others, remaining active in Europe until about the time of the American Revolution. Other plagues and poxes followed in its wake.

The Black Death and other epidemics particularly ravaged the medieval Catholic Church. In this period the Church provided the only medical care in Europe except that of "barbers," who cut hair, trimmed beards, and conducted "bloodlettings." The medical care provided by the Church was very primitive. No one in the fourteenth century had any knowledge of microscopic germs, sanitation, hygiene, or other medical concepts that we take for granted today. Few Europeans even understood how basic organs like the heart and stomach worked. In many cases the only real care available was having someone provide you with a comfortable bed, warm food, spiritual care, and wet cloths to control a fever.

It was in this climate that the Church confronted the Black Death and dozens of other diseases like smallpox and cholera. It was to the Church's credit that the sick and dying were brought to its doors for care. The European clergy reacted nobly and rose to the challenge, but they also paid the price. While one in four Europeans died of the Black Death, almost one out of every two (approximately forty to forty-five percent) Catholic clerics died from this particularly virulent disease. It is likely that another ten or fifteen percent lived but suffered horrible physical ailments after surviving the illness.

These statistics are even more grim when we consider that some areas of Europe (Ireland and Poland, for instance) were barely touched by the Black Death. This means that the areas where the Black Death hit were likely even more seriously devastated than the statistics show. Death counts were extreme and often created Beau Geste-type scenarios where monks and nuns carried out their duties to the last surviving person. Some scholars even recorded that in many villages nobody was left to bury the last person who died.

It is likely that in many areas between fifty and eighty percent of the Catholic clergy fell victim to the Black Death. This had a dramatic effect on the Catholic Church. First, missionary efforts to new countries were brought to a standstill. The emperor of China had requested Catholic missionaries, but there were none to be had. Massive efforts now had to be made just to preserve the teachings and structure of the Catholic Church in Europe.

This was not easy to do. Books were rare, and religious doctrines were mainly passed by word of mouth. The teaching of religion was therefore severely hampered when many of the older, more experienced clerics fell to the Black Death. These were generally the "veterans" who trained the next generation of priests and nuns. This hurt the effectiveness of the Church for decades to come. It was at this time that many of the problems of the pre-Reformation Church arose.

More and more of the Church's efforts had to be diverted from evangelization and preaching the truth, to just plain caring for people. There were fewer and fewer clerics to provide care for the sick and the orphaned, just at a time when these groups dramatically increased in size. During this period there were no printing presses, so books, Bibles, and religious works had to be written by hand. It was a labor-intensive task, often done by scratching letters on animal hides and darkening them with lamp black. Because of epidemics, the production of Bibles and religious materials became scattered and less effective. This hampered the teaching of the Catholic faith.

During this period, leading up to the Reformation, the Church suffered heavily by not being able to properly train its religious clerics in the teachings of the Church Fathers. Imagine what it would be like if we in the modern era had few books or methods for conveying the teachings of Christ. Our main method would be oral or verbal — that is, by word of mouth, through songs, and plays. For teaching tools we would have a few statues, a few paintings, and images in stained glass. Now imagine that about fifty percent of the religious of all denominations died suddenly and another twenty percent became invalids. What would happen? How could the faith be spread?

This is the type of scenario that the Catholic Church faced throughout most of its existence leading up to the Reformation. Destruction of the Church's framework came in many forms. In the tenth and eleventh centuries, for example, the Catholic parishes of England, Ireland, France, and Scotland were decimated by Viking raids. In other centuries the parishes of Central Europe were ravaged by the Huns and Magyars. In the 1400s the parishes of France were uprooted by the Hundred Years' War, which was actually a succession of wars lasting from 1337 to 1453. The Mediterranean areas were being ravaged by Moors, Turks, and Saracens. On top of it all, the European continent was constantly under the pressure of famine and disease, one of the most horrific being the Black Plague.

It is in this light that we see the devoted Christian effort of the monks, nuns, and priests of the Catholic Church. It is to their extreme credit that they did not flinch in the face of hardship. Instead, many millions died or became incapacitated while caring for their less fortunate brothers and sisters in Christ. ‡

The sheriff grabs the Jesuit, thrusts the lantern in his face,
and makes him swear an oath . . .

CHAPTER TWO

Jesuit Lies

~☙~

What Brian is about to do may cost him his life. It is the year 1588 and Queen Elizabeth sits on the English throne. It is late at night. He stands in the shadows of a dock at the Port of Plymouth, England. A feeling worse than that of being a hunted spy comes over him as he watches the queen's sheriff and fifteen armed deputies waiting on the pier. They are looking out into the fog-choked harbor, waiting anxiously for the vessel *Galway* to come to port. Someone has tipped them off. The situation will likely turn deadly if the *Galway* reaches her destination on time.

It begins to spit rain. The drops are cold and sting his face, but Brian smiles all the same. The dismal weather is perfect for the occasion. God has blessed his mission with cover to escape. The fog will also provide him with the perfect excuse to sound the horn that he is holding at his side. He raises it to his lips and blows hard. The horn's deep booming call is muffled a bit by the fog, but it echoes across the harbor. There is in the distance a responding call from the *Galway*. Brian shudders as he realizes his mistake. He called on his horn in hopes of concealing his efforts if the *Galway* made it to the pier. Unfortunately, his call has acted as a guide for the unwary vessel. He waits for disaster.

The fog soon parts and the vessel silently slides into sight. She looks like a ghost coming out of the darkness and clouds. The *Galway*'s crew sees the pier and begins to go into action. Barefoot sailors start yelling and scurrying as sails are dropped and the vessel moves into the dock. The sailors are skillful and the docking occurs without incident. The tension rises as Brian prepares for disaster. He raises the horn to his lips and lets out another long blast. The tension in his body subsides as his lungs' contents pass through his horn.

A gangplank is dropped from the ship and soon passengers begin to disembark. The sheriff and his men wait at the edge of the walkway. They form a curtain of drawn swords to prevent anyone from escaping. Two men with matchlock muskets also watch the water in case anyone tries to escape by swimming. The trap is ready; the quarry must now be flushed from hiding.

The burly sheriff watches and waits. He lets the women and children pass without much thought except to verify that they are such. The men from the boat, though, are all stopped and questioned. Seeing this, Brian pushes forward to listen and be ready to help. He is almost certain that his life is over. He is only an unarmed carpenter, but he must help if he can. The sheriff holds a lantern up to each man's face as he grabs him by the shirt and spins him around. He makes the men swear an oath to God that they will tell the truth. He then asks the question "Are you a Catholic priest?" to each of them as they pass. Each man reacts differently. Most are scared, but they all give the same response.

If the sheriff feels they are lying, they will go to prison, possibly to be tortured for months. Brian strains in the darkness to see his priest-friend, but he is nowhere to be found.

Maybe he is still hiding on the ship. Maybe he chose not to risk his life in England. Brian must be ready though. If the sheriff grabs the priest, it could be disastrous. But what does he look like now? Brian hasn't seen him since he left England to become a Jesuit priest some five years before. How will Brian know that it is him?

The Jesuit had once been a promising bureaucrat in a northern shire, or county. He had the government's favor, wealth, and a comfortable job. He was pursued by women but had retained his virtue. That was before Queen Elizabeth was crowned monarch of England and supreme head of the Anglican Church. Things then changed dramatically. The Jesuit had been fined for not attending the queen's church services. When he still refused to comply, he was removed from his government job and his lands were forfeited to the state. He still refused to submit to the queen. Things were certain to get worse. That was when his dear friends persuaded him to flee to France, where he could worship in freedom. He decided to do so but also to become a priest. Years had passed and he had now chosen to return. Everything depended on Brian identifying him quicker than the sheriff, but how? Brian puts the horn to his lips and blows as hard as he can. Maybe the Jesuit would hear his signal.

The sheriff continues questioning the men. The line gets shorter and shorter. Time is running out. What will Brian do? He prays that his friend has missed his boat. But Brian sees him in line, only four people from the sheriff. The Jesuit is staring Brian in the eye and smiling. He is not afraid. He knows Brian is there. He knows that Brian has seen him. Brian will be his guardian angel. Brian brings the horn to his mouth and readies to blow. He hopes that his dry lips will not fail him in his hour of need.

The sheriff grabs the Jesuit, thrusts the lantern in his face, and makes him swear an oath to God that he will tell the truth. He then demands, "Are you a Catholic priest?"

The Jesuit replies as he turns his head away from the light and brings a hand to cover his face from the sheriff's spitting voice. He says sternly, "I am not a Catholic priest . . ." Brian blows his horn loudly as the Jesuit covers his mouth with his hand and whispers up his sleeve ". . . who defies the pope." The ruse has worked, his words go unnoticed. The sheriff is convinced. He sets the Jesuit loose and confronts his next suspect.

The Jesuit moves on. Though he is an ordained Jesuit, he is dressed as an English merchant. He casually stands on the dock for a few minutes and watches as the sheriff completes his duties. The sheriff is certain that someone is lying, but he cannot arrest the whole crowd. He decides to board the vessel and continue his search. Brian blows his horn again and starts walking toward the town. The priest follows silently but purposefully, staying about fifty yards to his rear. Brian is so happy and excited that he can barely stifle the giggle that is welling up in his throat. His priest-friend has made it ashore!

Twenty minutes pass. Brian walks by an alley where Richard sits in a horse-drawn cart. Richard takes the horn from Brian's hand as Brian walks silently on into the darkness. A casual glance to his rear shows the priest climbing aboard with Richard. The first part of the mission is over, seemingly a success. Brian is unaware of the terror that waits ahead.

A month has passed since Richard has taken the Jesuit to his home. It is a fine dwelling, where Brian has prepared a secret room for the priest's safety. Brian dares not visit him though. His friend has assumed the dangerous role of a Jesuit priest, heading an illegal and clandestine Catholic parish in the heart of Elizabethan England. The Jesuit is having a dramatic impact. He has been illegally hearing confessions, baptizing children, confirming adults, and conducting Catholic weddings and funerals. He has now even become so bold as to begin actively recruiting parishioners from the queen's church. It is an extremely dangerous move as the enemies of Catholicism are everywhere.

On occasion he has been seen on the streets of Plymouth, recklessly reading a Catholic Bible and counting Hail Marys on a rosary as he contemplates the mysteries of Christ's life. An urge to greet him is quickly suppressed when Brian realizes that spies may not only be watching the Jesuit but also Brian. A careless act could spell doom for everyone. Things are exceedingly quiet, like the proverbial calm before the storm.

A few nights later, there is a terrible pounding on Brian's door. Fear overcomes Brian as he braces himself for the worst. His relief is immense when he finds out that it is only his friend Richard. But Richard is anxious as he recounts a tale of terror that began two nights before. A new convert had joined the parish just after Brian's Jesuit friend had arrived. The convert was overly zealous, almost to the point of drawing attention to himself in his efforts to make the acquaintance of everyone in the parish. That was when the Jesuit had requested that they treat him with caution. He ordered that he be isolated from the rest of the parish. Luckily, the convert never found out that Brian was secretly a Catholic.

Two nights ago, the convert had come to Richard with the tearful tale that his wife was dying and that he urgently needed "the priest" to give her the Last Rites before she expired. Richard had been torn by the fact that the Jesuit had been waiting nearby in the secret room, listening to the entire tale. Richard wondered whether to reveal the secret room and immediately send the priest with the convert. Fortunately, he had used extreme discretion by telling the convert that he should return to his home to comfort his wife. Richard had confided that he could contact the priest, and the Jesuit would be there shortly. Reluctantly, the convert left, heading directly to his residence.

At this point the Jesuit had emerged from hiding. Richard had urged him not to go, being fairly certain that the convert had no wife. The Jesuit refused. Since every day in England was a risk to his life, how could he falter now, especially at the risk of a young woman's soul? The priest grabbed his holy oils and threw on his merchant's garb. He crossed himself as he opened the door and stepped outside. The Jesuit turned silently and whispered, "Richard, pray for me!" as he pulled the door closed and slipped into the shadows outside. His voice held a mixture of courage and fear. Richard was exhausted but had been afraid to sleep. He gathered what little money and portable possessions he could carry and sat in a chair that had a view of the street leading to his house.

Four hours later the door burst open and Richard was aroused from a deep but fitful sleep. "Hide!" the priest called to Richard, who jumped up from his chair. The Jesuit turned and bolted the door. "It was a trap!" he muttered as he seated the wooden bolt securely. Richard had tumbled to his feet and come down the hall in time to see the priest opening the shutters on the back window.

The Jesuit grabbed Richard's suitcase and threw it on the lawn outside. Then he opened the door to the secret room. "They are after both of us, Richard!" the priest whispered as he pushed him inside. Richard called for him to join him in the secret room, but the Jesuit refused. "They have dogs . . . the dogs have my scent!" he puffed, being almost out of breath. "They will find me in the room . . . and you too if I join you!" With that the first hound could be heard barking outside of Richard's front door. The priest kissed his rosary and tossed it to Richard as he triggered the closure of the secret door. "Richard, if I go with you, the dogs will find both of us!" he said. "Pray for me!"

The dozen or so men at the front door had circled the house and closed in for the kill. They made quick work of the entryway with their axes and took the Jesuit without a fight. "Where is your friend?" the men demanded as they beat the priest.

"My friend is probably in Le Havre by now!" the priest replied, referring to a friend living in France. The hounds were given a robe from the suitcase on the lawn and ordered to chase Richard. The dogs were confused because Richard's scent was in every room in the house. The scent also led out to the lawn and outhouse. Chase was futile. Richard was safe. The posse soon gave up and took the Jesuit to the sheriff. Richard had waited two days in the secret room, and he was now with Brian.

~ঞ৯~

The two huddle in the darkness of Brian's front room. They are afraid to light a lamp for fear that Richard might be seen. Brian feels that he personally might be beyond suspicion or the sheriff would be visiting him by now. The two consider their options. The queen's agents will certainly torture their Jesuit friend. If he cracks, it will spell everyone's doom. Luckily for Richard, the queen's men think that he is gone. But Brian and his family are at extreme risk. The queen's torturers are known for their efficiency. It is certainly only a matter of time before Brian is exposed.

The hours turn into days. The days turn into weeks, and the weeks into months. The Jesuit has not cracked. Brian's family is safe. He wonders if the priest has survived the torture and the months in prison. The Jesuit's fate is finally known when Brian hears two men in the market joking about the next day's events at Meade's Hill.

"Two Jesuits are going to be given the opportunity to take the Oath of Supremacy," they cackle. "It should be quite a show!" Brian almost vomits in disgust. He hurries home to his family and his friend Richard. Soon the entire household is sick with tears. The evening passes and no one eats. That night no one sleeps. When morning arrives, Richard and Brian make the long walk to Meade's Hill.

It is a sunny day, with crowds gathering for the morning's entertainment. There are vendors and tents. People milling here and there, jugglers juggling, and musicians playing minstrel songs. The carnival atmosphere is broken by the martial sound of drums being beaten slowly as a cart full of men moves forward to the gallows stand that marks the hill. The wagon is led by a dozen officials on horseback. It is followed by a score of the queen's musketeers. The Jesuits sit in the cart beside two burly men. The Jesuits wear blindfolds; the burly men wear masks. The masks guarantee anonymity and protect the men from clan reprisals. Eight horses are led behind the cart. They are rigged with plow harnesses and thick ropes.

The carnival atmosphere has been destroyed as the gravity of the situation rings home. The officials dismount and climb the gallows. They address the crowd with tales of the greatness of Queen Elizabeth and the terrible deeds of the Jesuit priests and their Spanish accomplices. "Spanish accomplices?" Brian whispers to Richard in disbelief as he looks for his Jesuit friend.

The speeches continue as the Jesuits are led up the gallows stairs and pushed to center stage. They limp weakly as if their leg and hip joints have been knocked out of place by some cruel torture. As they hobble forward, the harnessed horses are led to positions at each side of the gallows. At this point Brian notices the horse handlers have bullwhips in their hands. The masked men standing next to the Jesuits also brandish large axes and carry butcher's knives in their belts.

The speeches end. The drums roll and both Jesuits are unmasked. They stand defiantly, but they blink their eyes as they adjust to the sunlight. The priests are temporarily disoriented but quickly gain their composure and stoically await their fate. Brian does not know the older Jesuit but immediately recognizes the younger one as his friend. He is a sad sight; his beard is several inches longer and his appearance is totally unkempt. His face is bruised and scarred, and many of the teeth that made his smile handsome are now missing. He stands quietly as if he is praying. Brian cannot tell because the Jesuits' hands are tied behind his back.

Brian silently prays for them himself. He is afraid to make the Sign of the Cross because it would immediately mark him for arrest. Brian prays hard, though, as both Jesuits are placed standing on stools with nooses around their necks. The official announces that they both have been convicted of the "terrible crime of being Catholic priests." He adds further that the queen would like to express her munificence by allowing the priests the opportunity to recant by taking the Oath of Supremacy.

The oath is then read to the older Jesuit. It calls for the respondent to recognize the monarch's role as supreme head of the Church of England. All religious affairs will be derived through her, not from the pope or the Bible, the accused are reminded. The oath is read in its entirety and the silent crowd waits for the elder Jesuit's response. Affirmation of the queen as head of the Anglican Church will mean his freedom. A negative response will mean his slow death by torture.

The crowd waits silently. The tension grows as the elder Jesuit begins to speak. He stutters for a second and looks around. "Friends!" he calls with a sorrowful and penitent tone. "The proposition that the queen of England is the supreme head of the English Church . . ." — he pauses as he gathers his composure — ". . . is laughable!" He begins to speak again, but his voice is cut short by the sound of the chair being kicked out from beneath his feet. He plunges some four inches as the rope tightens around his neck. The fall is not enough to kill him nor break his neck but designed to slowly choke him to death. His eyes bulge and his tongue lolls out as he begins to spin a bit. His skin turns red and then blue as he passes into unconsciousness.

As the priest hangs there, one of the executioners strips off the victim's garments as the other pulls out a long butcher knife. Two men hold the naked Jesuit up by his armpits as they release the tension on the rope. The knife cuts the rope and the Jesuit is held higher. The loosened noose allows air to return to the priest's lungs. He is awakened by pain as the knife is then used to cut away all signs of his manhood. The

Jesuit tries to scream, but the partial hanging has crushed his voice box.

The executioners throw him facedown onto a chopping block. An ax is raised and his head is hacked off, which hits the gallows floor with a sickening thud. His severed head is raised on a pole for the entire crowd to see. His body is then raised and cut open, the internal organs being drawn forward onto the gallows, in the manner of a hunter field-dressing a deer. The crowd gasps at the savagery. Brian almost throws up as the stench hits his nose.

The corpse is then lowered so that the limbs can be tied to each of four horses. The ax men position themselves to be ready. Horns blow and the "bullwhipped" horses pull in different directions as the ax men swing at the torso. The body is ripped to pieces as the horses begin to run out into the fields. The elder Jesuit is no more.

The carnival is over. Terror has set in. The crowd is somewhere between shock and mayhem. Horns blow and guards call for silence. The official on the gallows then turns to Brian's Jesuit friend who has just witnessed this horrid spectacle. The Jesuit knows that this will be his fate if he does not comply with the wishes of the queen. The drums roll. The official reads the accusations against the Jesuit. Brian closes his eyes as the Oath of Supremacy is read. Brian's mind is spinning as the oath comes to its end. He waits in terror for his friend's reply.

The Jesuit then speaks. "Pray for Queen Elizabeth . . ." — he calls to the crowd — ". . . that she will return to God's true Church." Brian sobs silently to himself as he hears the chair being kicked from beneath the Jesuit's feet. Richard and Brian turn and walk away. They cannot witness the spectacle that is about to be repeated.

A week later Richard leaves for France to start training as a Jesuit priest.

Jesuit Lies?

Much is written in English history about Bloody Mary and the Spanish Inquisition. Little is written about the English, Irish, Welsh, and Scottish Catholics who were "hanged, drawn, and quartered" by English monarchs who claimed to be the supreme head of the English Church. Between the reign of Henry VIII (1509-1547) and about the time of the birth of Thomas Jefferson (1743), there were almost a thousand such executions. This period spanned some two hundred years and included an average of about five such executions per year. Thousands of other Catholics were fined, exiled, impoverished, imprisoned, or tortured for clinging to the Catholic faith. Many others migrated to the Americas or other parts of Europe to escape persecution.

Initially Henry VIII and Queen Elizabeth required all subjects to obey the Act of Supremacy and take the Oath of Supremacy recognizing the English monarch (and not the pope) as head of the Church in England. Failure to comply meant imprisonment, torture, and death. King Henry VIII also confiscated Catholic Church property and hand-selected the leadership of his English Church. An armed rebellion against these policies was defeated by the king. After that, resistance became more subdued. The Catholic Church in England slowly went "underground," with priests secretly moving from home to home, often living in secret rooms or hideaways. Many of the faithful also left for France, where they could be trained in the Catholic faith and return to the

British Isles to minister to Catholics clandestinely. During some short periods it was legal to be Catholic, especially if the monarch was Catholic. During other times, Parliament or non-Catholic monarchs outlawed Catholic priests "under pain of death."

The Jesuits belonged to a priestly order that was one of the most daring and successful in resisting the efforts of the various English and Scottish monarchs. The Jesuits were therefore vilified by English authorities, whose claim that the Jesuits were "trained to lie" was designed to inflame the general populace against the priests. The theory was that you could not trust the Jesuits' arguments to join the Catholic Church because they were so evil that they were trained to lie and mislead people. The exact opposite was true. The problem that the Jesuits faced was that they felt it was a sin to lie, especially under oath. This was terrible for them because the English legal system allowed officers of the law and the courts the ability to make people testify against themselves under oath. For a Jesuit, an honest answer could mean a death sentence and destruction of an entire parish. The Jesuits therefore proposed various ways to be truthful in a manner that deceived an officer of the law. The most common being to loudly make a statement and then retract it with a following whispered comment. It was a sad commentary about the times that a Jesuit would have to resort to such efforts to protect himself, his co-workers, and his flock from torture and extermination. ‡

The knight draws his sword
as he prepares for battle . . .

CHAPTER THREE

The Sacking of St. Michael's

Thin wisps of smoke pour outside as the Dominican priest forces open the door of St. Michael's Church. His companion, a Knight of Malta, drops his visor and bursts forth into the vestibule. His sword is drawn and he is ready for battle. But the church is dark and quiet, the only sound being the loud echoes that the knight has created and the distant flutter of pigeons escaping through broken stained-glass windows.

The church is empty. The priest and the knight cross themselves as they enter the main aisle that leads to the altar. The dramatic scene tells the story of the chaos that must have taken place some two days ago. The pews have been piled together and burned, statues smashed, Bibles ripped apart, stained-glass windows shattered, and the altar broken in two pieces. Hanging above the ruined altar is a dead priest, dangling from a candle wheel with an executioner's rope about his neck. He has died quickly, unlike the poor vicar that was found earlier in the churchyard well.

The knight moves forward and cuts down the dead priest, the body falling into the waiting hands of his Dominican colleague. They lay his body reverently near an undisturbed nativity set. The clay and straw figures of Jesus, Mary, and Joseph seem to look sadly down on the dead priest and his desecrated church. The Dominican blesses the dead body and says a prayer. It is a prayer that this region of France might find peace during these tumultuous times. The Dominican has only been a priest for three years, but since his ordination in 1560, he has officiated at burial Masses for more than twenty murdered priests, monks, and nuns.

"Huguenot- and Calvinist-controlled areas of France are no places for Catholic priests!" That was the warning that this Dominican priest had received from the mayor of the town he had visited that morning. The Dominican listened to the warning but knew that he had to meet with the Calvinists if he were going to convert them and bring them back to the Catholic Church. He would therefore have to go to the most active trouble spots and preach the Gospel of Christ.

On his way to St. Michael's the Dominican had run into his new companion, a Knight of Malta, who happened to be traveling in the opposite direction. When the knight found the priest traveling alone and unarmed, the knight insisted upon becoming the Dominican's protector. The Dominican refused this offer but to no avail; the knight was on horseback and could neither be refused or evaded.

St. Michael's was the second ransacked church building that the two had visited that day. The scene had been the same at each church. The clerics had been murdered and everything of value had been stolen. Plaster statues had been torn apart as precious jewels were ripped or pried from their settings. The same was true of Bibles and religious books. They were torn apart in an effort to get the intricately carved precious metals and jewels that were embedded in their covers and spines. The valueless nativity sets, which contained only graven images of straw and hay, had been left untouched.

The Dominican surveyed the scene at St. Michael's. All the religious flatware and candle ware, made of rust-resistant silver and gold, were nowhere to be found. The story was similar in regard to the valuable ornamental linens and stained glass that brought beauty to this once peaceful church. These too were now gone. The linens had been stolen and the stained glass shattered, the colorful pieces of glass being gathered up to be converted into cheap jewelry. The sacrilege of theft and murder at St. Michael's was further exacerbated by the desecration of consecrated hosts with human fecal matter.

The pair of travelers bury the dead. Then they make a few rudimentary repairs to the church in order to keep damage as a result of wandering animals and winter weather to a minimum. They also leave a note on the altar, describing the events as they saw them. This was done in case the two did not live to tell their tale. The companions then close the church doors and head to the nearest town. It is a fairly large trading village of approximately three thousand people. The town lies in the heart of Huguenot territory but has remained loyal to the Catholic Church and the king of France.

The journey is tense. Not only are they traveling on a road that is occasioned by bandits, but the whole region seems to be in the grips of a rebellion among the lesser nobles. Various barons have been chafing under the French king's taxes and onerous laws. The barons have even been rumored to have gone as far as leading troops of bandits in raids on the king's property and administrators of the king's law.

Two hours pass and the pair clears the wooded regions that surround the town. They see a mill and a stone wall. It appears to be a typical French community, its citizenry being made up of traditional Gauls, Celts, and the sprinkled remnants of invading Viking bands. The town, though, is extremely well guarded with vigilant soldiers who are armed with crossbows and fitted with armor. The sergeant of the guard is cautious and questions the visitors thoroughly before he allows them to enter. The guards are loyal to the king and as such are very careful as to whom they let pass through the village's gate.

Once inside, the travelers go to the local parish rectory, where they meet with several fellow Dominicans. They discuss the happenings in the region and talk with three ex-Huguenots that have come to the church for asylum. These individuals have made their confessions and have admitted to helping sack a remote monastery some five miles away. The men are sorrowful and fear for their lives. They know that the penalty for their crimes is death. If the king shows them mercy, they will at a minimum have their hands chopped off or be enslaved as punishment for murder and theft. It is likely that they will choose to spend their remaining years in asylum on these church grounds, the church property being beyond the jurisdiction of the local magistrates.

The Dominican forgives them and then asks where the other Huguenots are. He is told that the rest of the Huguenots are armed for rebellion and camping on the estate of a local baron, a German named Wolfram Rosche. The Dominican asks if the baron's followers are mainly other lesser nobles, merchants, and generally people of Germanic descent. The converts think a minute and reply in wonder that this was entirely true. The Knight of Malta is astonished too, as are the other Dominicans. The priest responds that this is almost certainly the case with the spread of Calvinist and Huguenot doctrines. These doctrines are generally only adopted by merchants, lesser nobles, and people descended from Germans.

The Calvinist doctrines are embraced by the Germanic Anglo-Saxons, the Dutch, the Danes, the Swedes, the Germanic Swiss, and various descendants of the Germanic Vikings but rarely by any non-German peoples. The Russians, the French, the Italians, the Irish, the Spanish, the Belgians, the Greeks, and even the various Mediterranean and Arabic nations have all rejected the Huguenot and Calvinist doctrines. The Dominican theorizes that the ideology must be something that is specifically contrived to fit the German culture.

He also notes that the merchants and lesser nobles have embraced it, but the peasants, scholars, and monarchs will not touch it. The Dominican wonders why this is so. He feels that the most confusing aspects of the doctrine are that pirates and bandits are some of the most disturbingly strong adherents to Calvinist doctrines. They have accepted the doctrines, though they do not reform their lives.

The Dominican and his companions discuss the issues further and ask the converts how they can make contact with the Calvinists. The converts hesitantly tell the Dominican that one of the Huguenots' most effective evangelizers will be preaching near the town's west fountain that evening. He will be distributing Bibles, they add, and looking for new converts. With that they hand the Dominican a copy of a Bible that has been printed in Geneva and smuggled into this part of France.

The Dominican takes the Bible and examines it, seeing almost immediately that it is quite different from the Bibles he has studied in the past. For one thing, his training has been done on Bibles that were handwritten on the rough parchment of sheep hides. This Bible, however, is printed on paper and produced en masse. He recognizes it as one that has been condemned and burned by the Catholic bishop of

Strasbourg. The Dominican comments that he has seen a copy of this Bible before and would like to take it with him to the fountain. The converts are as shocked as the Knight of Malta is at this brazen suggestion. The Dominican tells them that they should not worry because the "good knight" and an "angel of God" will be there to protect him. He then explains that martyrdom is not such a bad thing. He is not afraid to die for the Lord Jesus Christ.

Later that day, the Dominican and the knight excuse themselves and begin the walk to the fountain. It is a beautiful winter evening, but their thoughts are not concerned with the weather. The Dominican and knight are trying to consider the actions they will take when they meet with the Huguenots. The pair travels through narrow winding streets and soon turn a corner that opens onto a fountain and square. On the fountain wall stands a preacher holding what appears to be a Bible in his hands. There is a crowd of about forty villagers gathered around to hear his speech. They are extremely agitated and are responding loudly and vigorously to his calls.

The Dominican and the knight move forward, unnoticed by the crowd. They hear the Huguenot evangelizer condemning Catholicism, its practice of baptizing babies, its superstitions regarding relics and the Eucharist, its idolatrous statue worship, and its treatment of Mary and the saints as goddesses and demigods. The preacher then tells the crowd that the Catholic Church has been taken over by Satan and it is his personal tool for keeping people out of heaven. He explains that the Church's teachings will instead bring its followers to hell. The preacher now comes to a fever pitch and tells the crowd that the Church and its foreign leadership has stolen their property through tithes and collecting money in payment of sins.

The preacher wonders aloud how God will judge these villagers for letting the Catholic Church remain in their midst, now that the Bible tells us that Jesus will be coming in less than three years. He then links the king of France to the Catholic Church and tells the crowd that the king has no right to be their ruler. This brings a gasp from the crowd, as many know that their presence at this meeting has now put them in jeopardy of being imprisoned or executed for treason. The emotional preacher does not notice their response. He tells the crowd that they should not baptize their babies, pay tithes, or honor the king. He calls them to join him and his friends as they fight to rid the land of the "Roman" Catholic Church and control of the distant king who rules from Paris.

The preacher, though, finally realizes that he has moved too fast and his work has almost been undone by his call for open revolt. He sees the growing fear on the faces of his listeners. He stops for dramatic effect, then asks them to trust in the Bible. "If God is for us, who can defeat us?" he shouts to a rising chorus of male voices. "Do you want to be ruled by a French king and a bunch of godless Italians in Rome?" he baits the increasingly tumultuous crowd. Angry voices grow stronger and more intense. Many in the crowd are on the verge of rioting.

The Dominican has wanted to remain silent but fears that at any moment the crowd may lose control and begin a rampage that might destroy the nearby Church of Mary the Mother of God. The Dominican prepares to respond but realizes that he must wait for just the right moment before he rebuffs the preacher.

Again, the Huguenot preacher pauses for dramatic effect and then tells the crowd that they do not need priests, nuns, saints, or Mary. He also tells the mob of people that they do not need a king. The preacher holds the Bible on high and tells his listeners that they only need to read the Bible that he has given them and they will know what to do. He instructs them that it will show them that they must not baptize children. They must not let idols remain in their churches. They must not let the Catholic Church and king remain in power and, above all, that time is short because Jesus will be coming in just three years. He urges them that they must act now. He then further details that the Catholic bishops burn the Bible to keep people like them from discovering the "true path to heaven."

The Dominican can wait no longer. He intervenes with a calm but commanding voice: "The bishop burns these Bibles for good reason!" The crowd turns and becomes quiet at the sudden realization that a Dominican priest and a Knight of Malta are in their midst. The crowd has been so emotionally preoccupied that the two have remained unnoticed. The Dominican speaks further. He points out that these books are not really Bibles but political tracts that undermine the king and the Catholic Church. He holds the Bible on high and tells the crowd that no Bible in history has ever had a book called the "Epistle of Calvin." He also details that these so-called Bibles have notes in their columns that explain that the king of France is the Antichrist, and that the dukes of Savoy and Guise are two of the four horsemen of the Apocalypse.

The Dominican notes further that the Catholic bishops burn this edition of the Bible. They do this, not only because it is a politically motivated translation, but also because they had earlier purchased all the bad translations in an effort to remove them from the market. The printers, nevertheless, did not cease publishing the Huguenot Bible; instead, they raised the price and printed more copies in hopes of making increased profits. They hoped that the bishops would buy all the copies of the second edition too. The Dominican explained that the bishops decided that it was wrong to let someone profit from politically motivated translations of the Bible. They instead confiscated and burned this poor translation.

Everyone is silent. The crowd and the preacher show some discomfiture about the priest's comments, but before the Huguenot evangelizer can reply, the Dominican presses further. He relates that the preacher's teachings on Catholic statues, the saints, and infant baptism are only political tools to entice the crowd into rebellion and help the preacher and rebelling nobles economically.

The crowd begins looking suspiciously at the preacher, and a look of fear begins to spread over his face. The Dominican explains that the statues and paintings were one of the most vivid tools that the Church could use to teach religion to the uneducated people of the Dark Ages. He notes that it is true that the Book of Exodus teaches against idol worship but that it did not speak against "religious statues" being used to spread the faith. The Dominican points out that the Book of Exodus even stated that Moses put the tablets containing the Ten Commandments in the Ark of the Covenant, which was decorated with statues of winged angels. He also adds that the Book of Exodus shows that the Jewish people decorated their most sacred temples with statues of religious figures, this being done after the Ten Commandments were received by Moses.

The Dominican then states that the Calvinists and Huguenots are notorious for sacking Catholic Churches, destroying statues, and obliterating objects related to Holy
Communion. He goes on to say that their doctrines have only
been accepted in areas of Europe that are in rebellion against
a king or emperor. He notes that this is the case in Scotland,
Switzerland, Holland, France, and Bohemia. All these areas
are in rebellion and the rebels all embrace some form of Cal-
vinism. They sack Catholic churches, the Dominican explains,
to entice innocent people into rebellion. He states that once a
person is religiously tricked into destroying a church, he has
committed a crime (murder, theft, or vandalism) that puts him
under a sentence of death or maiming. The guilty person and
his family therefore have a vested interest in the fighting to
overthrow the power of the king. Their lives now depend on
the success of the revolution.

The preacher begins to try and refute the Dominican's
arguments, but he is shouted down and surrounded by the
crowd. The villagers call for silence as the Dominican begins to speak further. He states that infant baptism is totally
supported by the writings of the early Church Fathers who
knew the Apostles. He also tells the crowd that the Book of
Acts and First Corinthians state that "entire households" were
baptized by St. Paul and his followers. He then explains that
it is a good idea for adults to understand their faith and re-
new their baptism through the sacrament of confirmation,
this practice being similar to the biblical Jewish tradition of
circumcising infants and the celebration of Bar Mitzvahs when
the babies have become adults.

The Dominican, though, proposes that a revolutionary
could gain committed supporters by encouraging people not

to baptize their children. This in itself would be an act of rebellion against the laws of the Church and the king. Not only would this be an act of rebellion, but it would also be a well-documented act, since the parish priests keep detailed records of whose children are baptized and which ones aren't. All one would need to do would be to check church records to identify those in rebellion against the king. The Dominican then says that the Anglicans and Lutherans were all Protestants who were not in rebellion against their kings. All of these groups are ardent supporters of infant baptism. He wonders aloud why the rebelling Calvinists would interpret the Bible so differently from their "non-rebelling" brethren.

The Dominican then comments that the rebelling Calvinist nobles had a lot to gain by disparaging the need for priests, nuns, and monks. They would also gain a lot if there was no such thing as purgatory or the need to honor and venerate Mary and the saints. If these practices were considered pagan, there would be no need for religious clerics. There would also be no need for the Catholic Church to own massive tracts of land, including the land being currently used to support monks praying for souls in purgatory, priests saying Mass, or shrines and churches devoted to Mary and the saints. If these uses were evil, then these properties could morally be taken from the Church and given to the rebelling nobles. The Dominican argues that the nobles would then become rich at the expense of the Church and the peasants that were supported by the Church's social programs.

The Dominican's words have been very effective and the crowd is now preparing to treat the preacher with violence, but the Dominican calls for peace. He asks the townspeople to throw their "Bibles" in a nearby fire and not to harm the preacher.

The townspeople comply. The crowd then escorts the preacher to the gate and turns him outside. The preacher is taunted by many of the townspeople, who now realize that the preacher was using religious doctrines to trick them into rebellion. The Dominican then walks outside the gate to deliver a message. He tells the preacher that he as priest and confessor will be visiting the estate of Wolfram Rosche in the morning. He hopes that the Huguenots there will renounce their rebellion, return their stolen goods, and come back to the Catholic Church. With those words he blesses the preacher and returns to the village. The gates are shut and the preacher wanders off into the woods.

Everyone is happy that the Dominican has averted a crisis in faith and politics. Everyone is happy, except for the Knight of Malta. When the two return to the parish rectory, the knight confronts the Dominican. He will not let the Dominican go to Baron Rosche's estate. He tells the Dominican that there are hundreds of Huguenots there. If he and the Dominican confront the baron, they will both be murdered.

The Dominican replies that the good knight should not worry because as priest and confessor he will be traveling without the company of the Knight of Malta. This infuriates the knight, who tells the Dominican that he will not let him go alone.

The issue rages through the night until it is time to retire. The knight and Dominican are led to their cells and all is quiet. The two are soon asleep, sleeping the deep and restful sleep of those that have a clear conscience. When morning comes, though, all is not quiet. The Knight of Malta awakens to find that the Dominican has left on his mission of reconciliation some two hours before sunrise. The knight rushes to find his military equipment but instead finds only a note from the Dominican.

The note essentially explains the following points: that while the Dominican appreciates the efforts of the knight, the mission is far too dangerous; that one extra man, although he may be carrying a sword, will not impact the outcome of the meeting; that the issue is in God's hands, and sometimes acts of mercy and martyrdom open the door for a penitent heart. After he finishes reading the note, the Knight of Malta concludes that he may never see his Dominican friend again. A few days later the knight finds out that his deepest fears have come true. The Dominican never returns.

The Calvinist and Huguenot Rebellions

From the late 1500s through most of the early 1600s, most of Reformation Europe was racked with a series of wars, rebellions, and revolutions. Many of these violent events were linked with the rise of the Reformation and the impact of Calvinist and Huguenot teachings. During this period, major portions of Holland, Scotland, Bohemia, and Switzerland were ruled by unpopular foreign nobles from Spain, France, and the duchy of Savoy. Indeed, in many parts of what is now France, the king (from Paris) was seen as a foreign ruler who had recently taken control of a number of independent kingdoms that would eventually make up the country of France. All of these unpopular monarchs had their rule affirmed and blessed by the Catholic Church.

The common denominator of these monarchs was that their rule was unwelcome and their policies often clashed with the traditional cultures of the lands that they had recently wrested from local control. In Scotland the rich and highly educated French rulers looked down their noses at the uneducated and poverty-stricken nobles of the region. In Holland the Spanish monarch disregarded the traditional rights of Dutch nobles and merchants. He also forced Dutch families to house Spanish soldiers and mercenaries in their homes without just recompense.

This was not a sinister effort on the part of the Catholic monarchs who ruled these countries. It was simply the impact of the difference in cultures. It would be very similar to the people of the United States waking up one morning to find out that the president had died and the head of the Chinese Communist Party had inherited the president's position. The Chinese premier would likely have very little insight as to what was needed to keep Americans happy. He would likely act as he did in China and therefore infuriate the American people. He would then lose the next election. But what if there were no elections? What if the premier would rule until he died? What if he brought in others from China to help him administer the American government? What if the next person in line to inherit the presidency was also Chinese? What if his right to rule was justified by the Bible?

These were the issues that were facing Reformation Europe. The problem with these relationships was that the citizens had no way to get rid of an unfavorable leader. A monarch ruled by the "grace of God" and was born into the position. There was no way to get rid of a monarch short of assassination or armed revolution. Revolution was the choice of many who wanted to change the government in these areas.

The Catholic Church, however, vehemently preached against revolt and rebellion. The Church and the Bible taught

that bad monarchs were supposed to be endured and that
rebellion was against the will of God. The Church noted
that biblical characters and the early Christians had not re-
sorted to violence no matter how evil the pagan kings and
emperors had been. These Catholic teachings did not sit well
with those who wanted to promote rebellion against an unpopular foreign monarch.

The rebels who opposed the Catholic monarchs were
almost universally Calvinists or Huguenots. These doctrines
were ideal for their cause. First, if the Calvinist doctrines
were true, then it inherently meant that the teachings of the
Catholic Church were false. If this were so, then a monarch
consecrated by the Catholic Church and serving by the "grace
of God" had little legitimacy. His claim to be monarch was
severely weakened or nonexistent. Also, by portraying Catholics and the Catholic Church as evil and foreign, a revolutionary could rally support for the cause of independence. It
would no longer be the lesser nobles of Holland fighting
against the Spanish emperor. It would now be the Christian
Dutch fighting the evil Spanish of Madrid and the satanic
Roman Catholic Church. Men who would not fight and die
to protect the rights of nobles might gladly die to protect
their country and children from the forces of the devil.

Another factor would be that if Catholic teachings were
false, then Church lands and properties could be taken and
used for personal purposes. Lands could be taken and property stolen in a manner that would enrich the perpetrators
and weaken those who supported the monarch.

Would people use religion to gain freedom and undermine the power of a monarch? This was a major issue in
various parts of Europe, where pirates and bandits almost

universally proclaimed their Calvinist and Huguenot doctrines without abandoning their lawlessness or reforming their lives. In Geneva too, Calvin's doctrines were initially rejected by almost everyone. Calvin became disheartened and moved to other parts of Europe. A short time later, the people of Geneva revolted against the duke of Savoy. The duke in turn declared that the rebelling citizens of Geneva would pay the price by being executed for this crime. It was at this point that the people of Geneva embraced Calvin and called for his return. By doing this, they had a rallying point for revolt against a ruling monarch. The duke was now an "evil Catholic" whose right to rule lay only on his support from a Church that was proclaimed to be a tool of the devil.

In other parts of Europe, Calvinist and Huguenot mobs were destroying Catholic churches, killing priests, and stealing Catholic property. While there was little precedent for this in the New Testament or the history of early Christianity, it was a universal practice in Calvinist and Huguenot areas of Scotland, France, Bohemia, and Holland. Many people felt that mob rule was a tool for getting people to revolt against a monarch. As touched on earlier, if religious fervor led them to participate in such an act, then they would all be guilty of revolt, vandalism, theft, and murder. The penalties for these crimes ranged anywhere from torture and maiming to amputation and death. If a person therefore participated in these events, he had a vested interest in the success of rebellion against the monarch. As long as the monarch ruled, the perpetrator's life was in danger.

Adult baptism was also a useful tool for a revolutionary. If a person did not have his children baptized, he could easily be identified as one who was defying the will of the Catholic king. This was because Catholics followed biblical and early Christian practices of infant baptism. Since baptisms were recorded by parish priests, it would be very easy to find out who was defying the will of the king. One need only go to the local church and examine church records to identify a rebel. Here again, by urging only adult baptisms, a revolutionary was forcing a person to proclaim his defiance to the will of the king. This act moved a person into open revolt and helped commit him to having a vested interest in the deposition of a Catholic king. It is interesting to note that all the "rebelling" Protestant movements stressed adult baptisms despite the fact that the New Testament (Acts 16:15, 33; Acts 18:8; 1 Corinthians 1:16) states that entire households were baptized. Adult baptism is also in contrast to the Jewish custom of parents dedicating their male children to God by circumcising babies that are less than a month old.

It is also interesting to note that all the Protestant movements that developed in accordance with a Protestant king's wishes maintained that infant baptism was important. Orthodox and Coptic Christians follow this belief too.

The usefulness of Calvinist and Huguenot religious teachings as a tool for rebellion was noted by several monarchs and various religious officials. In France, Huguenots and Calvinists raised armies and navies to support their revolt against the king. Calvinists and Huguenots were therefore outlawed as rebels. When these rebel armies were defeated, Cardinal Richelieu made it legal to be a Calvinist or Huguenot in France. The king supported this effort because these groups were no longer a political or military threat. The cardinal and the king also realized that legalization of these denominations would ensure that religion would not be used as focal points for further revolution. As in all the Calvinist countries, once the threat of an unpopular monarch taking power decreased (mainly through the rise of democracy), the militancy of the Calvinists declined.

In other areas of Europe the Catholic Church and the Catholic monarchs had different levels of success against the Calvinists. They too generally viewed the Calvinist rebels with suspicion. During this period the monarchs and Catholic bishops rarely had messengers burst into their chambers with urgent dispatches saying that a group of Calvinist housewives were reforming their lives and holding a Bible study. While this happened on thousands of occasions, this boring news probably never reached the ears of those in authority. Instead, it was more likely that the monarchs and bishops heard other news.

Perhaps a messenger would rush into their rooms with news that Calvinists had sacked a church, killed a priest, monk, or nun, or accosted an official of the king. During the seventeenth century, people claiming to be Calvinists and Huguenots murdered thousands of priests, monks, and nuns. One historical account stated that over a ten-year period there was an average of one Catholic official being murdered every day in France alone. In other histories John Knox, leader of the Scottish Calvinists, openly boasted of his role in the murder of a Catholic cardinal. This was the kind of news that formed the monarch's and Church's opinion of the Calvinists.

The Church officials also observed that although the Calvinists claimed that the Bible was God's unerring gift to Christians for determining God's will, self-proclaimed Calvinists were not too particular about producing accurate Bible translations or using the Bible for political reasons. The

Church noted a dramatic flood of poorly translated Bibles, many with fewer books (or lesser in content) than in the Catholic editions. They also discovered that many of the Bibles came with notes claiming that certain Bible passages were disparaging references to specific political and religious individuals in sixteenth- and seventeenth-century Europe. It should also be pointed out that these "politically motivated" and "poorly" translated versions of the Bible have been abandoned by modern Christians.

The Church at first had trouble countering the arguments of the Calvinists and Huguenots, specifically because their doctrines were so new and they varied dramatically from person to person. As the doctrines became more definite, thousands of Jesuit and Dominican priests entered Calvinist areas and debated Calvinists in open and private forums. This was a fairly risky proposition because the Calvinists were located in areas that were in open rebellion against the king. Thousands of Jesuits and Dominicans were tortured and murdered for their efforts. They were in turn replaced by others who in the end met with significant success. Their main success was through refuting the Calvinist doctrines by showing that they weren't biblical or supported by the practices of the early Christians. The other successes were achieved by showing that many of the Calvinist doctrines were based on political, cultural, and economic motives. ‡

*The commissioner carefully notes
in his ledger all that he sees . . .*

CHAPTER FOUR

'The Secret Is in the Crust!'

The carriage's wheel slammed into a large rock and slid sideways, dropping suddenly into a deep rut in the muddy road. It was at that moment that the pie in the abbess's lap went airborne a few inches and bumped against a nearby pillow in the back of the covered carriage. Luckily, the pie was not much disturbed and she would be able to carry out the plan that had been proposed by her wealthy patrons. The abbess reached quickly for the pie, but as she leaned to grab it she froze, startled at what she saw on the far side of the cushion. At first she stared in shock, and then a tear came to her eye. The moment brought sadness to her like she had not known for months or even years.

As her vision focused on the canvas cover that protected the contents of the carriage she had noticed a patch of leather that appeared to have writing on it. The writing was in Latin and began with the phrase *"Pater Noster. . . ."* It was the "Our Father" written on parchment. She recognized the script, for it was her own. It was from the chapter of Luke in a Bible that she had begun transcribing when she was only a novice nun. How it became sown onto the side of the wagon, she did not know. It saddened her just the same and brought back joyous memories that were laced with the bitterness of events of recent times.

The nun picked up the pie and placed it on her lap. She held it firmly with both hands and then drifted off into a fog of memories about the abbey that she had once belonged to.

She remembered especially that fateful day when one of the king's commissioners showed up at her convent. The nuns had been somewhat apprehensive about his visit but felt that they had nothing to hide. They knew that they would make a good showing, and all two hundred nuns had gathered together to greet the king's representative with a chorus of holy songs.

The gentleman, though, would have nothing of it. He had barely gotten his coat off when the nuns had started singing. He was at first somewhat polite about it but then motioned to the abbess that he did not have time to be entertained by singing. It was autumn and the roads were muddy. He had traveled slowly and was now days behind schedule. He therefore could not wait on pleasantries and had to get down to business. He asked the abbess to dismiss her nuns and have them carry out their normal routines.

With that the commissioner pulled out a ledger, a quill pen, and an inkwell. He was not much for small talk but quickly commented that he noticed that the abbey appeared to be much larger and more prosperous than other properties in the area that were not owned by the Catholic Church.

"It is," the abbess replied truthfully. She told him that the property totaled some ten thousand acres and covered more land than any other property within a radius of twenty miles. The commissioner questioned further, apparently curious as to how this could be. The land was donated, she insisted. She explained that in about the time of the Viking invasions, one of the greater nobles donated the land to form the abbey. The area had originally been inhabited by the pagan Angles and Saxons. Centuries later, it was further colonized by the Norse Vikings.

The noble who donated the land had been an Anglo warlord who had converted to Christianity. He had then given up his warlike ways and wanted to bring peace to the area. This would be impossible, since the Germanic Angles, Saxons, and Vikings all subscribed to the Norse religions that involved the worship of pagan gods of war and chaos such as Wodan, Thor, and Loki. As long as the pagan Angles worshiped these Norse gods, there would be no peace or prosperity.

The Anglo warlord loved Christianity. He therefore set up the abbey to provide the resources for a grand missionary effort. The abbey would not only train people to teach the Catholic religion to his subjects, but it would also be a place for transcribing the Bible and for teaching aspiring students how to read and write. In the year 900 this would require large amounts of land. It took roughly six farmers to feed eight people in this part of Europe. This meant that to support two hundred nuns, the tract of land would have to be large enough for six hundred farmers to work and provide food for the inhabitants of the abbey.

There were other larger tracts of lands that were given to the various warlords of the time, but these had become smaller as the centuries passed. Each generation's passing generally meant that the estates were split between the land baron's sons, each estate generally chopped up so that each son could have an equal piece. After this happened over eight hundred years, the property of the barons had become incredibly small. If it started out with thirty thousand acres, it would likely be cut into thirds three times for each hundred years. Over eight hundred years it could easily be cut into thirds eight times. This would mean that a tract of thirty thousand acres could now be split down into tracts of fewer than five acres each. The decreasing size of the estates would cause each neighboring baron to have a fraction of land, whereas the abbey still had its original ten thousand acres.

The abbess also explained that once the Viking invasions were over, the lands of the abbey had been untouched by war. It was sacred and neutral property. During the recent Wars of the Roses, which lasted from 1455 to 1485, the region's farms had been devastated by petty feuds. Fortunately, the abbey had been spared the fate of its neighbors: barns burned down, cattle and sheep scattered or killed. The abbess noted, however, that much of the abbey's cattle and livestock ended up being given to poverty-stricken refugees in order to ensure their survival during the war.

The commissioner pondered this account, and said, "Perhaps," as he turned and looked around the abbey. The nun watched as he stepped toward the walls and examined some linens that hung on the windows. He counted them and then wrote in his ledger the type of material and complete description of each tapestry. He also stated a monetary value behind each entry.

"Plateware?" He asked the abbess as he turned toward her. What he meant, the abbess did not know. "Do you have any gold or silver plateware?" he asked, a little more politely. "Perhaps candlesticks?" The abbess finally understood.

"Yes," she said, smiling. "We keep gold and silver as a reserve against famine or to pay for food and help in times of crisis." The abbess took the commissioner to the small shrine that lay at the end of an alcove, where a two-foot-tall statue of St. Augustine of Canterbury seemed to gaze on anyone entering. The statue was inlaid in silver, as was a similarly sized golden crucifix that hung above the shrine. The whole arrangement was lit by candles that were placed in a dozen silver candlesticks.

The commissioner seemed enthralled with the beauty of the valuable statuary. He stood for a moment and then moved forward and fingered each piece. He also examined the silver candlesticks that lit the room. "All this wealth," he muttered to himself as he pulled out his ledger and began tallying the contents of the room. "Do you realize the value of these precious metals?" he asked as he turned to the abbess.

"Very valuable," she commented with an agreeable nod. "Last year we melted down six of the candlesticks to help pay for the care of homeless people when a fire burned the village of Lee's Corner."

The commissioner did not appear to hear the comment. "Why don't you melt the metal down into coins?" he asked.

"Coins are of little value to us," the abbess replied. "They would just sit in storage. A golden crucifix can be used for teaching and to show the importance we place on Jesus' dying for our sins. The love of Jesus is obvious when you look at a crucifix."

The commissioner responded that the precious metals would be better used elsewhere. He also felt that the cross would be more pleasing to God without having a gold statue of Jesus on it, the gold statuary turning the symbol of salvation into a hated idol. The abbess disagreed and said that the statue of Jesus was not a hated idol but a vital part of the presentation. Not only did it vividly show God's love for man, she continued, but it distinguished the cross from the pagan symbols that were being used in Europe and the Americas.

"We especially needed the figure of Jesus in our early missionary efforts," the abbess commented. She explained that the Norse culture of the time was dominated with symbols that were similar to the Christian cross without the figure of Jesus. The Norse pagans worshiped Thor, their god of thunder. His symbol was a cross-shaped hammer that looked almost exactly like a Christian cross. The Vikings placed this symbol on walls and hung it on chains around their necks in an effort to receive the protection of Thor. If the nuns did not have a crucifix with Jesus on it, then the pagans would have thought that the nuns were worshiping Thor or working on Thor's behalf. They would not have known that the nuns had been motivated by a love of Christ.

"Perhaps," the commissioner commented as he turned and asked to see the livestock that were owned by the abbey.

The two walked through a candle-lit hall, exited the main building, and headed to the barn. "Is that a lead roof?" the commissioner asked as he turned back to look at the abbey. "It must be two inches thick!" he added like a boy who had found a hidden stash of candy. He pulled out his book and began writing and calculating the square footage of the roof and the amount of lead that it contained. "Look at the copper gutters!" he went on excitedly as he scribbled further. The nun looked at him with puzzled eyes. She then remarked that they used lead for the roof because it could be easily formed into long sheets that never rusted, rotted, or leaked. Once laid, the roof would only need minor repairs and would last for centuries.

"Perhaps," the commissioner muttered as he finished and closed his ledger. The commissioner then turned and looked out across the pastures and saw about a thousand sheep grazing in the pasture. "Why so many sheep?" he asked as he turned to the abbess.

"We use sheepskin to make Bibles," she answered. She then explained that throughout the abbey's history, paper and ink cost too much and had been in too scarce supply, so the abbey still used parchment made from sheepskins to write on. "Follow me," she said as she took the commissioner to the scriptorium, a room on the second floor of the abbey.

When they entered the room they found six nuns scratching letters onto sheepskin parchment. They were doing so with metal stencils, using a finished Bible as their guide. One nun looked at the finished Bible and scratched letters onto the parchment. When she was done she handed the parchment to another nun who rubbed a black substance into the marks that were engraved by the stencil. The stenciling gave the letters body and form, while the black material made the stenciling legible by contrasting it to the background of the parchment. Once this was done, a third nun proofread the page and handed it to the fourth to make corrections, which were made by scraping the parchment until the letters disappeared. The letters would then be stenciled again, then blackened for the last time. The two remaining nuns worked with the candles to provide the correct amount of light. They also cut the sheepskin parchment into four equal sections so that each cutting resembled a piece of paper.

The abbess said that it took one sheep to make four pages of parchment. A four-thousand-page Bible would require about one thousand sheep. Each sheepskin would need to be processed and readied for stenciling, the wool being removed and the leathery skin being treated with rough chemicals to preserve the finished product. She explained that the whole process took time and that a group of twenty nuns working nonstop could usually produce one Bible per year. This effort, she added, took up about forty percent of the resources of the abbey for the entire year.

The commissioner, however, was barely listening, since his eyes and mind had been caught by the glinting and sparkling of light dancing off the cut edges of precious jewels. The jewels were inlaid in the spine of the Bible that was used as the original source for the newly stenciled Bibles.

"Fantastic!" the commissioner exclaimed as he walked over and plucked the jeweled Bible from the young nun's hands. The abbess almost gushed at the admiration, for the Bible was partly her creation. She had helped stencil it when she was a novice. She had also helped inlay the jewels, which were the donation of a rich count. The count had visited the small shrine of St. Augustine and his prayers had been answered. He therefore donated the jewels for the upkeep of the shrine and abbey. When he died he also left more funds to support people who would pray for his soul in purgatory and to care for orphaned children until they reached the age when they could live on their own.

The commissioner anxiously wrote a description of the jeweled Bible in his ledger and then asked the abbess if there were any obligations that the abbey had to the citizens of the area. He knew that the monasteries and abbeys of England and Wales provided citizens with primitive insurance policies and retirement plans, these being available to those who chose to participate.

"Yes, we do, sir!" the abbess responded. "We provide food for over two hundred elderly people, and we care for another hundred orphans. Poor beggars are never turned away without soup or a cabbage or such." She added proudly that the abbey provided the only schools in the shire, plus the only hospital and the best inn for miles around.

"What are your obligations for road maintenance and the local defense?" the commissioner asked the abbess as he turned to a different page in the ledger.

The abbess thought a bit. "Well, sir, we as a landowner must provide for our own defense, there being no standing army or sheriff to protect us from bandits." She then noted that the abbey employed a half-dozen archers who mainly spent their time hunting game, as permitted by the king. She began to explain that on one occasion the archers provided deerskins for parchment when an anthrax epidemic had almost wiped out the abbey's population of sheep, but the commissioner cut the abbess short. He wanted to hear about roads and not deer hunting.

In regard to repairing roads, she told him, her abbey was responsible for planking all the main pathways that connected her property with those that abutted the abbey. This consisted of chopping logs and placing them over muddy spots in the road so that wagons and carriages could cross safely without getting stuck in the mud.

"You have done a better job of that than most," the commissioner commented as he made notes in the ledger.

"We also repair footbridges and operate the ferryboat that connects us with the lands of the duke of Elchester," the nun remarked, somehow feeling that she needed to prove that her abbey was being run properly.

The commissioner turned and looked around some more, walking halls and inspecting cellars for food and wine. He checked the smokehouse and even watched as food was handed out to the poor. The abbess watched as he mentally calculated the value of the vegetables and breads that were being handed out at no charge to the indigent and homeless.

"Does the bishop inspect your abbey?" he asked as he turned to the abbess.

"Yes, sir," she replied, noting that inspections were done about four times per year.

"Are there written records?" the commissioner asked.

"Yes, sir," came the somewhat bewildered response.

"Where are they?" came the final question. With the question came a sinister look that brought a shadow over the abbess's heart.

Soon the abbess found herself leading the commissioner to the library. The library was one of the largest in England, having over twenty-five books. She displayed them proudly, but the commissioner did little more than note the number of books and their location. He seemed obsessed with the bishop's inspection records, which were soon turned over for his approval.

The inspection records covered about three hundred visits by succeeding bishops that occurred over almost one hundred years. The bishop's written comments covered everything from how well the abbey's choir sang to the amounts and quality of vegetables that were given to the poor. Some were observations made about the rudimentary insurance plans that were developed at the abbey, and others were about the number of visitors that came to visit the shrine of St. Augustine. There were some negative comments too, including occasional discipline problems or infractions of the abbey's rules as required of the nuns.

The commissioner brushed quickly over the positive comments but wrote down anything negative, covering all infractions, and notes about one nun who had requested that she be allowed to reconsider her vows.

"This will do fine!" the commissioner remarked as he closed the bishop's record books and handed them to the nun. He scribbled further in his ledger and then asked for his coat. He was given his garment, plus some warm bread and a flask of wine for his return journey.

As the commissioner and the abbess walked to the abbey's courtyard, the abbess posed one simple question to the commissioner. "Is anything wrong?" she asked, sensing that the inspection tour had not gone well.

"Perhaps," the commissioner replied. "Good day," he added as he headed for his coach. He called for his armed escort to mount up and soon the party was on its way northward, traveling into an incoming fog.

Months passed, and the visit of the commissioner was almost forgotten. The nuns lived in peace and quiet until one day a royal courier arrived. He was accompanied by an official from the Exchequer's office, the official in charge of the collection of the royal taxes. To their rear came forty mounted horsemen, all wearing the royal insignia and ready for battle. The visitors pulled into the courtyard, the Exchequer official's carriage parking in front and the mounted soldiers taking positions to the rear. The royal courier motioned to one of the horsemen, who pulled out a large horn, which he blew vigorously until concerned nuns and the abbess began to appear.

With their arrival the courier ordered the abbess to have all of the nuns and employees of the abbey come to the courtyard to hear and witness an announcement of a very important royal decree. The nuns stopped whatever work they were doing, then moved slowly and quietly to the courtyard. Once all were present, the courier read the royal proclamation.

It stated that by the wishes of his royal person, the king, and by act of Parliament, all monasteries and abbeys participating in superstitious practices, immoral acts, homosexuality, and so forth, were by royal decree ordered closed and their properties forfeited to disposal by the crown.

The echoes of the courier's announcement had barely ended as the amazed nuns looked at one another and whispered words of astonishment. Silence soon followed, the only noise coming from the horses or the occasional call of a distant bird. The silence became uncomfortable. The abbess finally moved forward to the official's carriage. She moved slowly and purposefully, curtsying as best she could.

Then she whispered to them so that only the official, the courier, and the captain of the guards could hear. "This is terrible . . . scandalous," she said in a low voice, pausing to study their eyes. "To think that a monastery or abbey would operate in a scandalous enough manner to provoke the wrath of the king and of Parliament." She paused again and then asked quietly, "Which monastery is being closed?"

The Exchequer's official, the courier, and the captain all chuckled among themselves. Finally, the official leaned forward as if to whisper in the abbess's ear. "All of them!" he blurted out, so everyone could hear.

When the shock was over, the nuns and the abbess complained that it must be a dreadful mistake, for there was none of the reported offenses at their abbey, nor those of any that they had ever visited.

The Exchequer's official laughed and spoke condescendingly that the abbess should not worry, for she would be well taken care of. With that he stepped out of the carriage and pulled out the notes of the royal commissioner. They detailed the location of all the abbey's valuables, which were soon under the watchful care of the official.

The astonished nuns were all taken to the main hall where they were informed that some of them would receive pensions, and others would be offered positions elsewhere in the Church. The abbess, though, questioned the sincerity of the official's motives. "If we are corrupt, why would you give us pensions? Why would you offer us other jobs in the Church . . . and by whose authority?"

The official, caught by the obvious insincerity of his offer, replied: "Do not question the generosity of the king." With that the abbess was confined to her quarters and then removed to a nearby village.

Two months had passed and now she was journeying back to her abbey. She was riding in the carriage of the abbey's new owner. She was carrying a pie in her lap, now completing the most important mission of her fifty-six-year-old life. She looked down on her pie admiringly, smiling at its contents. It contained no fruits or meats or cinnamon and other spices. It contained only a flowering of parchment. Each parchment was rolled and inserted in metal cups that were baked into the pie's outer crust so that they pointed outward like flowers coming out of a vase.

Her admiration of the pie ended as she approached the abbey. Her eyes were then drawn outward to the main building. She saw smoke rising from the courtyard and saw that the lead roof that adorned the hall was now gone. She wondered if the revolt of the peasantry and the northern barons had reached this far south, but the revolt was in defense of the monasteries and would likely not result in their destruction. She pondered this question and surveyed the landscape to look for any signs of war or rebellion. She could find none. She considered this issue as her carriage pulled under the archway and came to a stop, almost in the exact location that was used by the Exchequer's official.

She now was a foreigner and a guest at the abbey. Unfortunately, it was no longer an abbey but an estate of John Hawthorne. She stepped out of the carriage and watched sadly as workers tended a large fire. The fire was made from the roof support timbers of the abbey's great hall. The lead roof was now gone, having been dismantled and brought in sheets close to the fire. The fire was burning vigorously, its heat being used to melt the lead from the roof that it once supported. The workers skillfully applied their craft as they drained the melted lead into casts that created lead bullets and cannonballs, the finished product being loaded onto a nearby wagon for use by his royal majesty.

The abbess looked sadly at the destruction but was soon led into the main building by a butler who used to work as a gardener at the abbey. He was very friendly and courteous to the abbess, much in the manner that she had been to him since the day that he began working for her.

As they moved through the estate she noticed that all the copper guttering was gone, as were the fine linens. The furniture too had been either broken up or auctioned off. All of the statuary and pictures were gone. It was as if the place had been picked clean and barren.

She begged the butler's leave and asked to be taken to the abbey's small shrine of St. Augustine. The butler agreed but pointed out that she would not be pleased with what she found. Once at the site of the shrine, she understood. The shrine was gone, its outline still shadowed — from the soot of hundreds of votive candles being burned daily over the centuries — on the wall where it had provided protection. The soot-free silhouette standing out against the wall as fateful testimony to hundreds of years of devotion was all that remained. The silver statue of St. Augustine was now long melted down and the golden crucifix desecrated in a similar manner.

The abbess shook her head sadly and then began to walk away. As she left she passed the scriptorium, where her nuns had translated hundreds of Bibles over the centuries. She stuck her head in the door and found what she had feared so much. Her hand-stenciled, jeweled Bible — her pride and joy, the signature event of her years as a nun — lay ripped apart and scattered on the floor. The spine of the Bible lay there, permanently damaged by the use of knives to pry loose each precious gem. The pages of parchment were scattered and flung about the room. The nun sobbed silently at the loss and examined the Latin text that lay strewn about on the floor.

"They use the Bible's parchment for repairs, madam," the butler spoke up with a note of deep gravity in response to her unasked question. He further explained that the pages of leatherlike material were being used to patch holes in everything from mattresses to shoes, from draperies to carriage covers.

"I know," the abbess said quietly as she picked up one of the pieces of parchment and motioned for the butler to take her and her pie to see John Hawthorne.

In a few minutes they were in the library standing in front of Mr. Hawthorne. He seemed a likable man, a man of wealth who enjoyed many of the pursuits of a country gentleman's life. However, he seemed concerned at her presence and acted as if he could not keep his eyes off of the parchment pie that she held in her hands.

"Welcome to my estate," he said confidently as he motioned for her to take a seat. She did so, putting the pie on the desk in front of him. "What have we here?" he asked. She did not reply to his question but first thrust the torn Bible parchment toward him and asked what had happened to the numerous Bibles that had been destroyed in the scriptorium.

John Hawthorne replied that he did not know, the books having been torn apart before his arrival. He noted, though, that with the availability of ink, cheap paper, and modern printing presses, there would soon be plenty of Bibles in England. The loss of one did not matter much in the bigger scheme of life. The abbess disagreed but did not say so, since she believed that it would be futile to argue with one whom she was hoping to peacefully negotiate with to obtain concessions.

"What are you here for?" he asked finally, wondering what the purpose of her journey was.

"I am here to trade you this abbey for the contents of this pie," she responded as she pushed the pie closer to him.

Mr. Hawthorne put the Bible parchment in his lap and leaned over the pie. He looked suspiciously at the rolled parchments that protruded toward him. "What is this?" he asked cautiously as he plucked a parchment and carefully unrolled it. "Property deeds?" he exclaimed quietly as he pulled one parchment after another and placed them on the table and then in his lap. "What are these for?"

The abbess explained that the parchments were a form of "bearer deed" entitling the holder to all rights of the property. She remarked that many of the local barons were willing to donate land to Mr. Hawthorne in exchange for his turning over the abbey to the abbess. "These are prime properties," the estate owner muttered, trying to understand why someone would donate so much wealth to the abbess.

"Are you willing to trade?" the abbess asked. Mr. Hawthorne pondered the question for a bit and then asked the abbess to step outside to give him ten minutes to think things over.

The abbess complied and soon the butler was escorting her back into the room. The words "It is impossible" cut through the nun's hopes. He calmly pushed the pie back to the abbess and then curtly handed her the Bible parchment that he had laid in his lap.

"Why not?" the abbess asked softly. "Is it not a great deal?"

Mr. Hawthorne whispered softly that such a deal might cost him his life.

"Cost you your life?" the nun asked again, not believing her ears.

Mr. Hawthorne motioned for the butler to shut the doors so that the two of them could speak privately. After the butler left, the estate owner explained that the king had given the monastic properties to his favorites to shore up support for the crown. The king feared being overthrown. He had recently almost bankrupted the royal finances in a long, expensive, and disastrous war with France. Losing the war had cost the crown its last French possessions. Not only was the king unpopular, but he had no male heir, and no support for raising taxes for his government. It was likely, Mr. Hawthorne added, that the government would topple. To add to the king's problems the Catholic Church was blocking his efforts to divorce his wife and marry another. The abbess wondered what this had to do with the king's confiscation of monasteries and abbeys.

Mr. Hawthorne further explained that the lesser nobility and armed knights were becoming restless and that all of England feared a second rendition of the costly Wars of the Roses. The abbess finally began to see what was going on. The closing of the monasteries was not some terrible mistake but a calculated transfer of wealth from helpless landowners to those who were armed and might cause trouble. Mr. Hawthorne agreed but stated that it was much more serious than that. Not only had the monasteries been targeted because of their wealth but also because they controlled so much power and were only responsible to the pope and not the king. Several abbots, as landowners, even had seats in Parliament, their vote possibly serving as a veto on the king's ability to raise taxes and formulate policy.

The abbess understood the reason for the confiscation of property, but it did not prevent her from posing this simple question: "Who will look after the poor?" She noted that the sick and the lame, the orphans and widows, the homeless — all these unfortunates no longer had anyone to look after them. Monastery schools had been closed because the new landowners would not support them. Charity in the countryside was withering and dying.

"This is true," Hawthorne stated matter-of-factly, "but the country is now better defended than it was. The royal finances have been restored, and the king has purchased the loyalty of the nobility." He stopped for a minute to think before continuing: "In regard to the peasants and the poor, they are on their own." He then talked of the need for cheap labor to work in the new factories and mines. He talked of royal statements that questioned if manual laborers and farmers really needed an education to do their jobs. He then stopped, suddenly realizing the gravity of it all when he began thinking of poor friends of his own.

"What of honoring the saints and praying for poor souls in purgatory?" the abbess asked, wondering about the fate of those who had passed before her. Mr. Hawthorne responded that the king was currently attacking veneration of the saints and the concept of purgatory. He added that if veneration of the saints and praying for souls in purgatory were not seen as false or superstitious, then the whole concept of confiscating the property of the monasteries would be seen as totally unjust. On the other hand, he went on, if such veneration and supplicatory prayers were seen as superstitious or unneeded, then the seizure of the monasteries' lands and treasures by the royal family could be easily justified. The king could argue that the property had been obtained by the Church under false pretenses. He would then be a hero for returning it and its wealth to the crown and the landed barons.

After some thought he expressed his belief that the numerous holy days in honor of the saints were bad for business because workers were idle and markets were closed. This might be fine in an agricultural society, he observed, but not in an industrial one.

The abbess finally understood. At one point the king had been the ally of the Church. He had now turned against Catholics to satisfy the financial and political needs of the royal House of Tudor. He had confiscated monastery lands throughout England, and if anyone rebelled, be he an abbot or a duke, he would be executed.

Mr. Hawthorne was very kind to the abbess but soon had her — and her pie — escorted back to the carriage. The abbess was saddened but not undaunted. She returned to the village and retired to her room that had been provided by her grandnephew in his home. Once there, she began preparing a schoolbook for first-graders. She had received a modest pension from the king and was using the balance to finance a one-room schoolhouse. Children would learn to read there in the day while the homeless and widows would use it as a home at night.

Years later the nun would hear that King Henry had died. With that news came word that he had left a small fortune to support those who would pray for his soul in purgatory. His will and testimony also left money for the establishment of a church in honor of the Virgin Mary. The abbess read this and did not know whether to smile or cry.

The Suppression of the Monasteries

Many people have heard the following *Mother Goose* nursery rhymes without understanding what they really meant:

"Little Jack Horner"
Little Jack Horner sat in a corner,
Eating a Christmas pie.
He put in his thumb and pulled out a plum,
Thinking "Oh, what a good boy am I."

"Sing a Song of Six Pence"
Sing a song of six pence,

A pocket full of rye.
Four and twenty black birds
Baked in a pie.
When the pie was opened,
The birds began to sing.
Now, wasn't that a dainty gift to place
To set before the king?
The king was in his counting house
Counting out his money,
The queen was in the parlor
Eating bread and honey.
The maid was in the garden,
Hanging out the clothes,
Along came a blackbird
And snapped off her nose.

Both rhymes are said to be regarding the suppression of the English monasteries by Henry VIII. They also refer to the Catholic efforts to defend the monasteries or have them reopened.

It was a strange belief of the time that if you gave a gift to someone important, it was considered much more impressive if you "baked it in a pie." This is somewhat similar to the habit of wrapping presents in "gift wrap or paper" in modern times.

In the first rhyme, "Little Jack Horner," a Catholic abbot sent a pie full of deeds to King Henry VIII. The messenger carrying the pie reportedly went by the name of Jack Horner. He also reportedly could not resist taking one of the donated properties for his own. He did this by stealing one of the deeds from the freshly baked pie, the deed supposedly being to the Manor of Mells near Somerset, England.

The second rhyme, "Sing a Song of Six Pence," was also reportedly regarding an abbot's efforts to comply with Henry VIII's confiscation of the monasteries. The blackbirds in the rhyme are representative of deeds for the twenty-four monastic properties. As you can see at the end of the rhyme, the king and queen were extremely wealthy from the proposition, but the poor laborer (the maid) was treated rather harshly by the blackbirds. This was fairly similar to what happened in England, the rhyme being representative of the money that the royal family gained at the expense of the laboring classes and the poor.

Monastic Wealth in the Sixteenth Century

In many European countries the Catholic Church controlled between twenty and forty percent of the country's wealth. A modern person might question how and why the Catholic Church would have gained so much wealth as to control, say, forty percent of a European country's economy. The main reason for this was that the European Catholic Church in many instances provided most of the services that are offered by modern governments and businesses. For instance, in fifteenth-century Europe the Catholic Church generally provided all or most of the following services: medical care, education, scientific research, operation of libraries, provision of retirement and insurance plans, engineering services, religious courts, operation of inns, royal ambassadorships, reproduction of manuscripts, protection for travelers, police protection, freeing slaves, caring for refugees, and patronage of the arts.

As you can see, these efforts required the collection and

transfer of large amounts of wealth. In modern economies these services are provided by governments and businesses (with some still being offered by the Church). The efforts might take up resources that would require between twenty and forty percent of the economic resources of a country. They are paid for by customers or through tax collections by local or federal governments. In medieval Europe these services were provided by Church officials but paid for by tithes, donations, and the produce of ecclesiastical (or Church) lands.

A modern person might wonder why the Catholic Church had chosen to take on these tasks, especially since most modern churches do not do them, and neither did the first Apostles of Jesus. To understand this, we must remember that particular part of European history when the Christians at the time of the Apostles were basically an "illegal underground Church" until about the middle of the fourth century. As an illegal underground Church they could not provide these services on a large — and public — scale.

In later years Roman Emperor Constantine converted to Christianity and legalized the Catholic Church. From that point in time the Church began to become "publicly established" and groups of clergymen started to band together in religious communities to follow God. They also began to establish hospitals and orphanages.

Shortly, thereafter, the western part of the Roman Empire (which covered most of Roman Europe) began to come apart under pressure from the barbarian invasions. When the Roman Empire fell, the barbarians did not come to replace the empire's leaders but to destroy the empire and take its wealth. Villages and cities were burned and plundered. Men and women were murdered or carried off as slaves. All major cities, including Rome, were left abandoned. Roman society was totally destroyed. Traditional learning ceased among the citizens of Western Europe.

Society was totally destroyed, that is, except for the Catholic Church. It is an amazing fact that the barbarians left the properties of the Church relatively untouched and almost totally intact. This was done in part because one of the main barbarian leaders had a vision commanding him not to touch the Church's properties or priests.

This miracle left the Catholic Church in an incredibly awkward position. Its goal was to convert people to Christianity, but now it was also being called upon to perform many of the societal functions that were described above. This was because the barbarians had basically destroyed the infrastructure of Western civilization. Within a couple of generations after the fall of the Roman Empire, there were few non-clergy adults that could read or write, nor could they communicate in a tongue other than their own. This was because the barbarians who now ruled Europe had little skills other than farming, irrigation, ironworking, navigation, and the use of simple tools.

When they conquered Europe, the barbarians had few people who could read or write, repair Roman roads or aqueducts, and so forth. While a barbarian could easily tear down a column or an arch, he could scarcely figure out how to build or repair one or how to build a harbor that would protect ships from storms. The barbarians also had little capability to correspond with other countries, since they did not know how to write or speak in a language such as the universal language of Latin. The members of the Catholic Church, though, had access to books that could teach all these skills.

The Catholic Church was able to successfully convert the barbarians of Western Europe from paganism to Catholicism. But to do this and provide the social services as described earlier, the Church would need resources. In many barbarian lands coins (or paper currency) were practically nonexistent. The main source of wealth was not in money but in land itself. Land was donated to the Church in great quantities by the newly formed nobility of Western Europe. Charlemagne himself was a great patron of the Church and donated a large percentage of the German lands that he had conquered to the Church to help missionary efforts there.

These Church resources were used to dramatically improve living conditions in Western Europe in the Dark Ages. Not only were the lands vastly improved under the care of technically advanced monks, but with the use of these lands Christianity began to flourish. While paper was in short supply, Bibles and catechisms began to be inscribed on sheepskin, which had been rendered into parchment. Hospitals were developed and libraries were established. The poor were cared for (as best as possible under the circumstances) and the sick comforted. Europe began to move forward and escape many of the problems that were inherent to being conquered by barbarian invaders.

As years turned into centuries, the landed barons became more and more jealous of the properties of the Church. While the monarchs still gave strong support to the monks and nuns in the monasteries and abbeys, the poorer knights and barons coveted their lands. This was because of the decline in social status that was being seen by knights and lesser barons across Europe.

With the passage of time, knights became less and less important. Catholic monks had brought gunpowder to Europe. Its explosive power had later been harnessed for military muskets and cannons that now made mounted knights relatively obsolete. The knight's sole role in society had been the defense of the nation. Because of gunpowder they were now playing a lesser and lesser role in this function, their importance being replaced by trained soldiers who worked as musketeers in direct pay of the crown. The knights and lesser barons were therefore dramatically in need of a way to reassert themselves both economically and politically.

In the end, the monasteries' main problem was that their own success was becoming their undoing. They were so successful in reestablishing a Western civilization based on Christianity that the newly civilized people could now carry out the roles that the Church had assumed. A king no longer needed a multilingual cleric to help him carry out foreign policy. This was because the monastic schools and Catholic universities were now producing plenty of promising nonclerical bureaucrats who could perform the same tasks. The king no longer needed monks to conduct engineering work, lay out harbors, or develop aqueducts because the Catholic education system was now producing laypeople to complete such tasks.

The social and economic needs that were being fulfilled by the monasteries were now capable of being realized by secular forces. What the monarchs and barons wanted, though, was wealth, and many of the monarchs and barons saw the monasteries as an incredible source of wealth that could be used for their own purposes. Remember that since banking was in its infancy and the minting of coins still done on a relatively small scale, the monasteries not only had valuable land but were repositories for jewels and precious metals. Since there were no banks, the monks often turned the precious metals into religious statuary and plateware so that it could serve a useful purpose instead of lying in a trunk or buried under a rock for safekeeping. The question, though, was: "How could an unscrupulous monarch simply take the Church's wealth?"

While many of the functions of the monasteries could be done secularly (printing, education, retirement plans, insurance, etc.), there was no legitimate way that the king, barons, or dukes could claim to be able to operate shrines or celebrate Masses and conduct prayer services for the dead. How could a monarch or baron therefore claim "consecrated land" or "holy items" and use them for his own purposes?

This was the question facing many monarchs in Europe. Many who coveted the Church lands chose to discredit the Catholic Church and its teachings in order to justify seizing Church property. First, they claimed that there was no purgatory, so then resources related to supporting those who prayed for souls in purgatory could be taken. Second, they claimed that veneration of the saints was an invalid and superstitious act. Once this proposition was accepted, then all shrines and Church lands devoted to the veneration of saints could be confiscated. All gold and jewelry normally donated to shrines in thanks for heavenly favors could now go to the king instead of for maintenance of the shrine or for the aid of the poor in time of need. Third, monarchs and other rulers downplayed the possibility that things could be "holy or consecrated." This allowed them to use sacred objects and properties for their own purposes.

On a final note, if the officials of the Catholic Church were portrayed as hopelessly corrupt, then the property that was used to support their various works could easily be taken from them. To do this, the kings and barons would need proof. Lacking proof they would need crimes where no physical proof could ever be found; this gave rise to claims of monks being involved in sexual immorality and superstitious acts like idol worshiping.

In England, Henry VIII was the first to come up with the idea of confiscating the Church's monastic properties. He saw this as a way of replenishing the royal treasuries, shoring up support from his lesser nobles, and of weakening the power of the Church as a counter to his absolute rule.

Other European monarchs and princes watched with eagerness as Henry VIII seized the properties of the English monasteries. Princes in Germany and Scandinavia began converting to Lutheranism and claiming Church property as their own. In Scandinavia, several warrior-princes openly stated that they were converting away from Catholicism so that they could take Church resources and use them to finance their war against Denmark. The leader of Denmark soon did the same thing so that he could use Church resources to even the odds.

In Germany, Martin Luther had an assistant named Melanchthon. According to William Durant in his book *The Reformation* (MJF Books, 1957), Melanchthon stated that the German princes did not care about religion but were instead motivated by greed, pointing out that "they do not care the least about religion, they are only anxious to get dominion in their hands, to be free from the control of the bishops; for a slight alteration in their theological garb they escaped from the Episcopal taxes and courts, and could appropriate pleasant parcels of ecclesiastical property."

He goes on to say: "Under cover of the Gospel, the princes were only intent on the plunder of the Churches."

The story was similar throughout Europe. Church property was being taken and devoted to personal use. Not only were schools and hospitals closed, but the concept of venerating saints and praying for the dead came under extreme attack. The practice of caring for the poor was abandoned too.

The plunder of Church property also increased the tempo of European anti-Catholicism for centuries beyond the death of Henry VIII. The main issue revolved around the thinking that if Catholic doctrine and tradition were ever seen as correct, then the closure of the monasteries would be indefensible. It would also be likely that the properties that belonged to the now rich nobility would have to be returned to the Church. This would impoverish the nobles as it had done when the emperor returned confiscated Church lands to the Catholic Church in Germany in the early 1600s.

When this was done in Germany, anti-Catholic propaganda increased dramatically in England. Verbal attacks on the Spanish Catholic heirs to England's crown increased dramatically, and wild tales regarding the Spanish Inquisition were printed in droves. The motivation for the attacks was that the English feared loss of property and wealth if the Spanish took over control of England, as appeared likely because of dynastic customs. During this period Catholics were physically attacked, executed, and their properties confiscated after trials were conducted on trumped-up charges of conspiring with the pope to "blow up Parliament" or "burn London."

The remnants of this anti-Catholic propaganda, related

to the confiscation of the monasteries in Europe, can sometimes still be seen even in the twenty-first century.

This chapter is dedicated to the selfless monks and nuns who fought against hardship and prejudice to further the cause of Jesus Christ. Be they the dedicatd monks and nuns who continued their work after the closure of the English monasteries, or those working in present-day Harlem and similar places, their testimony to Christian perseverance must be recognized by all who become aware of their efforts to help the less privileged brothers and sisters in Christ. ‡

*Sitting astride his fine horse, the
Janissary is a magnificent sight . . .*

CHAPTER FIVE

Gbur Is Visited by the Janissaries

~≈e≈~

They are coming for the children!" The urgent cry is whispered from wooden hut to wooden hut in the tiny village of Gbur. Fear has gripped this tiny seventeenth-century Balkan hamlet of thirty families. A wandering friar has just arrived with news that a troop of forty mounted Janissaries has arrived at the village of Naved, which is only six miles away. Everyone fears and respects the Janissaries. They are the sultan of Turkey's fanatic shock troops. The Janissaries are his favorite tool for spreading his rule by military force and also for administering the laws of the Ottoman Empire. Their proximity has ignited anxiety in the hearts of all the villagers.

The friar has relayed his story of how a tenth of the Christian children of Naved were being chosen for the special services of the sultan. The story tears the hearts of mothers, fathers, and elderly grandparents who remembered the visit of the Janissaries to Gbur some fifteen years before.

The Janissaries had come to Gbur in the autumn of the year, taking every tenth Christian boy and girl. The village had been devastated by the loss. Families had been shattered and parents' dreams destroyed. Brothers and sisters, sons and daughters —all had been "drafted" by the Janissaries and moved hundreds of miles to the Ottoman capital city of Istanbul. After a few weeks, the priests of Gbur had conducted a grand funeral for the lost children, for it was certain that they would never return. The drafted Christian maidens would become harem girls and slaves for the sultan. The Christian boys would become militant Janissaries, elite warriors in the conquering armies of the sultan. Christianity would be torn from their souls and replaced by the tenets of Islam; the young men would be trained to become fanatical Muslims.

The barefoot friar's story has brought sadness to the village of Gbur. Fathers look at mothers, parents at children, grandparents at grandchildren. Anyone who is old enough can remember that fateful day fifteen years ago when the Janissaries first visited the village of Gbur. It was about 1615, some eight years after the region's last Christian prince had lost this land to the armies of the sultan. The town was Christian and, as such, paid heavy taxes to the sultan. The tax collectors had arrived to claim their annual tribute, but this time it had been different. The collectors had been accompanied by a Janissary who paid special attention to the children between the ages of five and twelve. He was seen writing names on a tablet, choosing prime subjects to become tools of the sultan.

The next morning, a score of Janissaries arrived to take possession of the village's taxes — and the village's children. A few fathers resisted but were brutally slain for their efforts. The fathers had been defenseless against the well-trained Janissaries who fought with long bows and scimitars, curved swords favored by Turks and Arabs. The village had been filled with cries of terror as children were separated from their parents at the point of a sword or the tip of an arrow. Resistance was futile. The Janissaries left with both the taxes and the children. As they parted, they told the villagers that life would be easier if they would only abandon their faith in Christ. By doing so, they would pay less taxes and could keep their children.

That was fifteen years ago, and now the terror has returned. Sadness is everywhere as the villagers consider their fate. Some talk of armed revolt, but everyone knows that this is futile. How can thirty men armed with sticks and rocks defeat the cream of the sultan's army? Even if the villagers could surprise or overwhelm the Janissaries, it would only be a week or so before more of the sultan's forces arrived and destroyed the entire village and executed its inhabitants.

In the back of everyone's mind is the offer that the Janissaries will make before they take the children and the taxes. The villagers could convert away from Christianity. They would then be taxed at a lower rate and their children would remain with them as long as they pleased. This scenario is almost as heinous as losing their children. It is not seriously considered as an option by the villagers but tortures their hearts and consciences nonetheless. They are used to paying extra taxes as Christians (which is just part of life), but the choice of losing one's children if one keep one's faith in Jesus — this is an option that can drive one to insanity.

In either the case of "converting" or "remaining faithful," the children will be converted away from Christianity. What could one do? The villagers realize that it is all a devilish numbers game. There is a "one in ten" chance that one or more of their children will be selected. If their children are not chosen, the children can stay Christian and remain with their parents. To some, the odds really didn't seem too bad.

Other villagers reason that the best physical specimens among the children are the ones that are always chosen. They are the prettiest girls for the harem or the strongest boys for the sultan's army. Could the parents wait and see if their children were likely to be picked? If so, could they then mar their children's bodies in some fashion that would make the Janissaries choose another? The torturous options are almost overwhelming to the parents. The friar senses this and calls the villagers together on a local hill for prayer.

From this hill, the villagers can see the sun glinting off the cross of the steeple of St. Peter's Monastery. It is a day's journey away, but it stands in Christian territory. The sight of the cross shining in the sun brings peace to the minds of the villagers. They pray fervently. An hour passes, and the villagers feel consoled by their prayers but need only to look at their children to return to a state of morose sadness. After prayers are finished and baptismal promises are renewed, there is a period of silence. The friar asks that the children be brought together in a group for a blessing. This is done and the children are returned to their parents who hug and caress them as their most prized treasures.

The loving scene is broken by a call from the town's only merchant. He motions for silence and then asks the friar what they should do. Everyone agrees that converting from Christianity is as intolerable as giving up their children. They also agree that resistance is futile. The friar looks upon the pitiful sight of fathers and mothers who are certain that their perfect children are the obvious ones that will be chosen by the Janissaries. The friar tells the crowd that fighting is useless, but flight is possible. He warns that running from the sultan might be as deadly as standing to fight.

The crowd is both saddened and electrified by the idea. The villagers have a deep fear of travel. No one but the merchant, two hunters, and the friar have ever traveled more than three miles from the village. The village's peasants are legally tied to the land and not allowed the privilege to come and go as they please. They know that travel has its perils. There are certainly bandits to contend with, and, more certainly, mounted Janissaries who will hunt down the fugitive villagers as they flee for safety. But if they run, where will the villagers go? There will be no safe haven for them as long as they remain in the sultan's empire. The roads and borders are guarded by the sultan's troops, and the villagers will fall easy prey to bandits if they stray far from the main boulevards or try to hide in the woods. The villagers also wonder how they can travel safely with women, children, and the elderly.

The friar, however, has an answer. He points to the hills on the horizon where the land is still in the hands of Christian princes. The peasants can plainly see the distant steeple of St. Peter's Monastery on a hill some fifteen miles away. That is where they shall go, guided by the cross on the steeple. The friar tells the villagers that they must return to the village and eat and drink their fill. They will only be able to carry blankets and items that will fit in one hand or can be carried lightly in pockets or pouches. The village will be abandoned, their property and livestock given up to the first person to visit. Most likely their possessions will be lost to the hated Janissaries, but no matter, the loss of their homes will be a small price to pay to keep their children and their faith.

A few hours pass. The sun has gone down and the villagers have gathered in a group around the town's well. Everyone is present, even the elderly and the sick. They have followed the friar's instruction and have arrived with only food, blankets, walking sticks, and flasks of wine and drinking water. Several peasants carry religious drawings, statues, and crucifixes. They dare not carry torches or lanterns. The lights would be easy for the sultan's soldiers (and various bandits) to spot in this dark and fearsome country. Instead, the friar gathers everyone for prayer as they wait for the full moon to rise and illuminate their path to freedom.

The prayer is rudely interrupted by the unwelcome arrival of the first of the Janissaries. He has obviously been sent ahead to collect taxes and choose the children who will be pressed into service by the sultan. He has arrived on horseback and has stopped at the edge of the hamlet to survey the scene of the villagers gathered in the dark. The peasants cannot tell if the man is admiring them or wondering whether the assembly is somehow illegal. A shiver of fear mixed with a sense of guilt moves down the spine of each and every villager.

The full moon rises and illuminates the tense scene. The Janissary waits as he studies the crowd and the crowd studies him. He sits on a fine horse and is dressed in colorful garments from head to toe. His brown beard reaches to his chest. He wears some sort of white turban upon his head and a sash around his waist. He also carries both a scimitar and a long bow with a quiver of arrows. In addition he carries a flute that is pushed down into his sash. He is a powerful man, well armed for war. The crowd of helpless peasants realizes that he alone might be able to slay all the villagers if he realizes that they are about to flee.

The parents unconsciously pull their children close as the friar calls the Janissary forward in a friendly and welcoming voice. The Janissary is hesitant, seemingly confused by the gesture, but complies. He moves forward slowly, cautiously, with one hand on his reins and the other on the hilt of his sword. The friar welcomes him again and asks if the sultan's warrior is lost or needs food. The Janissary is indeed lost or, depending on one's perspective, is now found. He explains that he has been wandering in search of the village of Gbur. The villagers wonder if this is their chance to send the Turkish soldier on, but one of the children quickly and innocently exclaims, "This is Gbur."

The Janissary then dismounts and moves to the well for a drink. The friar bravely blocks his path and calls on him first to drink a toast to the sultan. Before the Islamic warrior can respond, he finds that the friar has given him a fist-sized cup and filled it with a strong drink that is much like whiskey. The Janissary is puzzled by this but cannot resist the toast as the friar raises his cup and swallows its contents.

The friar announces that the Janissary is here to collect the sultan's taxes. He then calls for the villagers to bring forward the taxes and drink a toast to the sultan. Confused, the villagers return to their huts and come back one by one to place their taxes at the feet of the Janissary. The warrior is puzzled by the fact that the villagers are depositing "about double" the taxes that are owed to the sultan. Each villager is also toasting the sultan with the Janissary as the taxes are being paid.

The Janissary looks at the taxes that are laid at his feet, then he looks off to the horizon. He stares for a minute, then notices the shadowy silhouette of St. Peter's. He appears hypnotized for a moment, then asks if there is a better place to view the distant monastery. The friar notes that there is, but that it cannot be reached by horseback. He then asks the Islamic soldier if he would like to be led to a hill where he can view the architecture more clearly. The Janissary agrees.

The friar takes the reins of the horse by one hand and grabs the arm of one of the village's hunters by the other. They walk toward a nearby barn as the Janissary begins to look around at the crowd. The parents notice this and again begin to subconsciously try to hide their children from his view. When the friar is out of earshot he stops and hands the reins to the hunter. He tells him that he is going to take the Janissary by a circuitous and confusing route to the hill. He will abandon him there and meet the villagers at a nearby fork in the creek in an hour. He tells the hunter to hide the horse and have the villagers on the road as soon as possible. If the friar has not returned to them by midnight, they are to leave without him.

The hunter, although anxious, agrees to the friar's plan. He and the horse then disappear behind a large wooden hut. With that the friar leads the Janissary off into the dark. They travel along a wooded and pathless route that crosses various ditches and ravines. To the friar's surprise the Janissary is extremely friendly — even quite trusting of the friar. And although he comments to the friar that it appears they are zigzagging a bit as they move to the hill, still the sultan's soldier follows the friar as if he were one of his flock.

A half-hour passes and the two arrive at the hill. Their skin is scratched from briars, but neither man complains. They walk on the hillside and search for a break in the trees. It soon comes, and the pair sit silently as the light in St. Peter's steeple illuminates the monastery's silhouette. "Magnificent!" the Janissary whispers under his breath. The friar is amazed that one could be so enamored with architecture. The friar too thought that the scene looked "magnificent," but his feelings were based on his love for Jesus.

"You can see better from that tree," the friar notes as he points to a mighty oak. The Janissary agrees and quickly moves to the oak. He pulls off his shoes and hands them to the friar. Within seconds the sultan's warrior has pulled himself up on the lower branches and is climbing upward. The friar looks up at the sky and watches the moon as it becomes cloaked by a long, puffy gray cloud. Darkness descends on the hillside and the friar uses this opportunity to disappear. He moves silently down the slope and deposits the Janissary's shoes in a nearby ditch. The friar is gone five minutes before the wind carries the Janissary's cries to him. He can barely hear them above his own panting breath, but he knows that the Janissary is looking for him. He must move on. To be caught now would mean that he would be beheaded.

At midnight, the friar arrives at the meeting point in time to see the last of the villagers move out toward St. Peter's Monastery. They appear only as shadows in the night, but he recognizes them all the same. The shadowy old man with the cane is Gulac the tailor. The child with the straw doll is Julia, the seven-year-old daughter of Joppe the woodcarver. The friar is encouraged but notes from a distance that they are moving slowly and noisily as they tramp through the undergrowth. One hunter is at the front of the party and the other takes up the rear. The entire group stops and gives a joyous welcome to the friar as he catches up with them from the rear. The villagers are both happy and anxious. They have gone beyond the point of no return. If they are caught, the best they can hope for is a quick death. They anxiously ask the friar about the Janissary, but the friar can say little to soothe their fears. He can only hope that the barefoot Janissary will wander through the woods until dawn and then find the village abandoned. At that point it will take hours to organize a pursuit. With any luck the villagers will have a ten-hour head start on a sixteen-hour trip.

But luck is not with the villagers. They are moving slower than expected through these thick and trackless woods. The woods are dark and people can barely see their hands in front of their faces, let alone the person in front of them. To prevent their being separated, the friar has had each person hold onto the back of the garments of the person in front of him or her. They now appear as a line of circus elephants holding each other's tails with their trunks. To make matters worse, they seem to be weaving as they walk. The hunters are good guides, but they must travel by the stars, although the stars are intermittently blanketed by clouds. The guides therefore are hesitant and follow a winding path.

Seven hours pass and the sun begins to overwhelm the darkness of night. Birds begin to chirp as dawn awakens the countryside. The hunters and the friar can now see that they are lost. They huddle for a bit, trying to determine their directions by examining moss on trees, looking at the sun, or feeling the prevailing wind on a wetted face. They soon decide that they must climb a nearby hill and look for the steeple of St. Peter's Monastery.

The party follows, and a half-hour later they are resting in a wood line that graces a grassy knoll. The hunters and friar search the horizon as the other villagers rest and breakfast on bread in a shady spot in the woods. The steeple is finally spotted. There is little relief though. The villagers have drifted miles to the north, and are much farther away from the border than they planned. The friar looks to his front and notices the river that they must cross to enter Christian territory. It looks far wider and much more treacherous than he had ever imagined. Several stretches of the river have white-water rapids, while other areas look ominously still and deep. The friar knows that few of the villagers can swim, and they have too few axes and too little rope to build enough rafts to get them across.

The friar looks to the north and notes wooden bridges that are guarded by both Christian and Muslim fortifications. That path is no good, since they would certainly be captured and executed before they could cross to the Christian side. The leaders consider moving to the south, closer to the way they came. Their conversation is cut short when the friar sees a horrifying sight that stops his conversation in mid-speech.

He has caught movement in the corner of his field of vision! His eyes are drawn back to the path that the villagers had followed the night before. They had crossed a muddy stretch of land that turned into waist-high grass and then gradually changed to trees that made up the forest. The area is about a half-mile away, but from his hilltop the friar can clearly make out the bearded, turbaned Janissary as he examines the tracks in the muddy field below.

Horror and panic run through the party as everyone realizes that the fanatical Janissary is hot on their trail. The shoeless man has cut his cloak in half and wrapped the pieces into makeshift coverings for his feet. He has also doggedly pursued the party through the woods in the night. He must have had difficulties tracking the villagers in the darkness, but the sultan's warrior has persevered. He will now be able to easily track the villagers by daylight. The villagers had been careless, their elephant-walk in the dark had left a beaten-down trail in the grass that a blind man could follow.

Seeing this, the friar watches in horror as he realizes that the villager's tracks point like a dagger to their present location.

The friar is horrified, but he does not panic. He asks the hunters to gather everyone up and lead them to a clear and rocky stream that flows down the far face of the hill. While he waits, the friar watches the Janissary as the man makes markings in the trail. The Janissary has counted the footprints in the mud and then made marks some ten yards apart. After making the marks, he paces along the trail twice and counts his own footprints. He is comparing the number of footprints he made in the mud, to the number of footprints that were there when he started. The cunning Janissary is trying to determine how many villagers he is tracking. If the villagers scatter, he will not quit looking for them until he has caught them all!

The friar watches further as the Islamic soldier takes out his scimitar and measures the length of several distinctive footprints. His experience has shown him that if the villagers cross a busy path, he will better be able to follow the people who made those particular footprints. The Janissary is both cunning and persistent. The friar now wonders how many of the villagers will die at the hands of the sultan's warrior.

Soon the hunters have the villagers gathered for the next move. They stand on a rocky area next to some tall grass. The grass extends for twenty yards and then enters an area that is covered with large hard-surfaced rocks. The friar has an idea. He has the villagers "elephant-walk" down the slope through the tall grass. When they hit the hard rock surface they head for the shallow stone-filled stream and begin moving uphill against the current. The friar watches as several slip on the rocks, but no one is hurt. They move quickly up the ankle-deep stream and are soon a hundred yards uphill.

The friar says a quick prayer and drops a string of rosary beads in the grass to better mark the trail. He then turns and follows the villagers as they journey some two hundred yards up the hill. When he arrives he finds that the villagers are moving on, but the hunter and a small girl still stand by the creek. They are searching for something. "My dolly!" she sobs. She has lost her straw-and-cloth doll.

They have searched but to no avail. There is no time to search further now, for the Janissary must be only minutes away. The hunter promises to carve a wooden doll for the girl, but still she cries. Frustrated, he places his hand over her mouth, picks her up, and carries her to her parents. The villagers move on, but the friar waits. He has to make sure that the Janissary takes the bait and follows the false trail down the valley below.

About ten minutes pass and the Janissary arrives. He walks stealthily as if he is afraid of being spotted. He scans the horizon in search of the villagers, and then looks to the ground for signs of their movement. Within minutes he has found the rosary beads and the villagers' trail through the grass. He studies the beads and then puts them in a pocket. He scans the horizon but sees nothing. There is confusion on his face. The villagers must be nearby, but he sees nobody. There is no place in the rock-strewn valley to hide so many people. The Janissary instinctively knows that he should be able to see them. He looks, wondering as he walks.

The Islamic warrior then decides to stop and rest on a nearby rock. He checks his feet. The linens on his feet make poor shoes. With each step he has left a drop of blood from feet that have been stabbed with sticks, cut with rocks, and blistered from ill-fitting linens. The Janissary adjusts the rags and then spies a piece of bread crust that has been dropped by a villager. He pounces on it and crams it into his mouth, barely chewing it before he swallows. The friar realizes that the man has probably not eaten in thirty hours.

Despite these hardships, the Janissary refuses to give up the chase. Instead he turns back to the stream and begins sipping water in a manner that reminds the friar of a deer he had seen at a pond some years ago. The friar's peaceful memories explode with a surge of adrenaline as he sees the little girl's straw-and-cloth doll float down the stream toward the drinking pursuer. The Turkish soldier sees it too and begins to look uphill as he rises to his feet.

The good friar does not wait any longer. He drops to the ground and crawls to a nearby ditch. He then runs to catch up with the villagers. He cannot make good time because the ditch is filled with vines and rocks and the friar is running in a stooped-over position.

Rain begins to fall. The villagers have traveled two miles, but the friar catches up with them, and the column proceeds with renewed haste. There is an urgent feeling of being hunted prey that drives the villagers. The young and the old struggle to keep pace and stay ahead of the feared Janissary. To stop and rest might mean certain death. The villagers find consolation in the fact that they have been traveling over rocky terrain, and that it is now raining heavily. The rain makes it harder to walk, but it helps cover tracks, muffles noises, and makes it more difficult to be seen.

Hours pass and the heavy rain continues. It does not slacken until the villagers reach the banks of the river that divides their province from the land of the Christian princes. At one point the river had been fairly dangerous but offered several safe places to ford. This is no longer the case. The river is swollen with the heavy rainfall that had helped conceal the movement of the villagers.

The peasants stand on the banks of the river, realizing that safety is only a stone's throw away. Unfortunately, they cannot cross, since the river has risen some four feet and shows no sign of falling. Logs and sticks drift by quickly and are tossed in the river's now deadly current. To cross by foot or boat would be senseless. The villagers' only hope is to find a bridge, but all the bridges are guarded and lay at least five miles away. They also realize that unless the Janissary is lost, he will be arriving within an hour or two. Death will certainly come swiftly and violently.

The two hunters have a few knives and sharpened spearlike sticks to defend the villagers, but their specialty is trapping with snares, nets, and pits, not fighting the elite troops of the sultan's army. The hunters consider their hopeless plan while one of the peasants, a woodsman, steps forward with a stone ax. He walks to a large tree and looks up, trying to guess how tall it is. Then he looks across to guess how far it is across the river. The friar and hunters realize what he is thinking and encourage him to start chopping. He does so in a manner that will drop the tree to the far edge of the river.

The loud *thok!* of the ax biting into the trunk of the tree begins to echo across the quiet valley. Anguish and excitement grow with each stroke. The villagers know that each swing of the ax not only opens the gate to their freedom but also certainly draws the attention of the Janissary that is hunting their party. The Turkish soldier is obviously a fanatic, desperately trying to stop them, as he knows they are so close to escaping. The hunters stand guard as all the men take turns swinging the ax. Fifteen strokes to a man, then they pass the ax to the next one in line. Within an hour, the villagers' hearts beat rapidly with anticipation as they hear the splintering groan of the oak, which is now leaning toward the river. Then *boom!* The great tree splashes into the tumultuous current.

The oak quickly submerges in the roaring water as branches break off and fly through the air. They crash into the water and are carried away as the main trunk of the tree reappears from beneath the treacherous current. The base part of the tree is fairly well anchored, but the tip has been pushed at an angle by the current. It no longer reaches the far side but stops some four feet short. The young and the elderly will not be able to pass.

This does not dismay the hunters, one of whom ties a fifty-foot rope around the other. When this is done, the pair walk to the middle of the tree bridge. The woodsman follows, clearing branches out of the way and forming a makeshift walking path. The path is clear, but it still allows the villagers the opportunity to grab various branches to support themselves as they journey across.

When the path is ready, the woodsman and one hunter hold one end of the rope as the hunter to whom it has been tied starts running as fast as he can. He heads fearlessly along the trunk toward the opposite shore. If he falls, he will likely be "reeled in" by his two companions. If he succeeds, he will be a hero to everyone in the village. Undaunted, he runs as far as possible, then plants his spear in the tree's bark. He tries to pole-vault into the air, but the bark gives way under his spear and the rope tangles on his leg. The hapless hunter flies skyward and then does a "watermelon" into the eroding bank of the far shore. He lies in the weeds for a minute, his still body not moving at all. The villagers wonder if he is dead, paralyzed, or just knocked silly. The woodsman pulls hard on the rope and drags the hunter's body back into view. This revives the hunter, who sits up and starts absentmindedly clawing mud, sand, and grass out of his hair and beard.

Within moments he is back on his feet and tying his end of the rope to a nearby tree. The hunter and woodsman motion to the friar to start sending the villagers across. The first peasants, with the help of the combination rope-and-tree bridge, cross the raging river and stand on the far shore, hugging each other and rejoicing in their success. Others follow with more difficulty. This group has many elderly and many children. The elderly have a hard time negotiating the passage, many being weak and feeble. The children and babies have a difficult time too. They must be cradled across the lap of an adult as the two hang beneath the rope, the adult holding on to the rope with his hands and legs as they move to the far side.

The majority of the villagers cross without any major difficulties, except an occasional dunking of feet and ankles in the river when legs slip away from the rope. The friar, however, does notice that as each villager crosses the tree bridge, his or her feet deposit a trail of slippery mud that the others must now negotiate. The crossing becomes more and more difficult as old men and young children slip in the mud. The friar is preoccupied with this problem, his efforts devoted to pushing the mud off the log with a stick. He is alarmed when the air suddenly becomes filled with the shrieks of women and the hoarse cries of men. The friar looks up to the river, thinking he may have to rescue a young child or grandparent who has fallen in the rapids. He sees nothing but notices that all eyes are pinned in fear to something that is standing directly behind him.

The friar turns quickly, almost slipping on the mud-choked bark of the tree. There, standing but fifteen feet away, is the dreaded Janissary. He is a terrible sight. His turban is torn and starting to come undone. The linens that wrapped his feet are nothing but soiled rags, the blood from his toes and heels flowing freely through the wounds. His fine clothes are dirty and tattered and his eyes and face are gaunt from lack of sleep and food. The only thing solid about him is his muscular frame, his scimitar, and the bow and arrows that are stored in the quiver on his back.

The cries stop and an eerie silence follows, the only sound being the pounding of the river's current on the branches of the fallen tree. No one moves. Everyone behaves like rabbits, frozen in fear. But more resounding in everyone's minds than the fear is the feeling of awe they have for this superhuman individual. The friar himself cannot comprehend what force would cause a person to relentlessly hunt these villagers to this river. Why would someone suffer the physical deprivations of exposure and hunger to keep a community enslaved and separate children from their families? Why would one man, though well armed and well trained, seek to battle a group of villagers such as these? The friar and the Janissary stare at each other. They look eye to eye, with just five yards separating them.

The silence is broken when the Janissary begins to walk forward. One of the villagers who has already crossed the river yells, "Run!" Instinctively, the crowd on the tree begins to lurch forward, but before any pushing or shoving can begin, the Janissary's loud voice booms out the command "Stop!" Everyone freezes in fear as the villagers realize that the Janissary has moved to within a sword stroke of the friar. The crowd's innermost hope is now that abject surrender might deliver mercy for everyone. The Janissary, however, has not grabbed his sword. Instead he reaches slowly to his turban and pulls it off of his head. Long brown hair drops to his shoulders as he holds the turban in one hand and reaches into his pocket with the other. He looks sadly at the friar with pleading eyes. Then he begins to speak. "I was once a Christian boy," he explains to the friar. Then he holds his hand extended on high and lets the cross of the rosary drop and dangle in the air just inches from the friar's face. "Please take me with you," he says softly, begging for mercy, almost crying. The friar explodes in tears of emotion. Not only are the members of the village of Gbur going to make it to St. Peter's, but one of the Church's children has come home.

The Catholic Church in the Age of the Ottoman Empire

It was a sad fact of the period between the twelfth and eighteenth centuries that both Christians and Muslims fell short of the teachings of God and treated one another dismally in the occupied lands surrounding the Mediterranean Sea. In both camps the treatment of subject religions varied according to the whims of the individual monarchs who ruled the land. In many instances various Islamic monarchs treated Christians justly, giving them relative freedom and the opportunity to practice their religion.

Under sultans like the Ottoman Turks, though, Christianity was persecuted with heavy taxes. The various sultans felt that those who refused to convert to Islam were not entirely loyal to the Ottoman Empire. The Christians were therefore held under suspicion and seen as a possible threat to the sultan's rule. They were a force that needed to be neutralized, yet kept strong enough to help maintain the empire. One solution that the sultans developed was to weaken the various Christian communities by "drafting" large portions of the strongest and healthiest Christian children. These children were taken to other parts of the empire where they were trained to be servants of the sultan, be they soldiers, administrators, or harem girls. The children would be raised with no family except the sultan. The boys would be sent to the far reaches of the empire and expected to fight and give their lives in the name of the sultan and militant Islam. The girls would be sent to Istanbul or the various governmental centers with the full expectation that they too would give themselves in service to the government.

In any case, the parents of these children were constantly faced with the dreaded question: Do we give up our Christian faith or do we lose our children? The question was answered over and over. In many cases, Christians tried to avoid the consequences of this choice by immigrating either as individual families or en masse. The choice was difficult and risky but accepted by tens of thousands of Catholics who wanted to remain Christian and keep their families intact. ‡

She leads the crowd in prayer
as the minister tries to tempt them with soup . . .

CHAPTER SIX

The Soupermen of Black '47

It is the summer of 1847. The night is illuminated by the dim light of a full moon. A family moves forward across an open field of tall grass. The seven of them are barefoot, dressed in tatters. The family's ten-year-old daughter treads carefully as she hugs her sleeping baby sister. The girl walks with her finger in the baby's mouth. The baby sucks gently but to no avail. The mother and father hold a ragged sheet between them as they walk purposefully toward a nearby bush. Their seven-year-old and five-year-old sons follow silently, carrying clublike sticks in their grubby hands. The parents' three-year-old daughter toddles deliberately behind as the family closes in on the shrub.

They are all gaunt, their ragged clothes hanging loosely around their bodies, each person being ten or twenty pounds under their ideal weight. Everyone is silent as the tension slowly rises. The family's survival is on the line. They creep forward on tiptoe as they surround the shrub and toss the blanket so that it covers the bush entirely. "Now!" the father shouts as he and his wife pull the sheet together on the far side. The boys pounce forward and beat the bush with all their might as they scream at the tops of their lungs. The baby cries and the toddler falls back on her bottom in fright.

Soon it is all over. Silence follows as the family gropes the torn sheet in search of a reward for their labor. They find nothing. Not even one solitary rabbit or bird.

The daughters begin to cry and the proud sons hang their heads in silence. Everyone is tired and in need of sleep. The father gives them words of encouragement as he looks to the sky. His words sound weak and hollow. The clouds move, and he begins to get his bearing by the stars. "This way!" he points south and west as he grabs his three-year-old daughter and puts her on his shoulders. The weight is almost too much for him. His head spins and he almost faints. He looks to his wife for help. He sees that her wrists are pressing the side of her temples to relieve the pain of a throbbing headache. The family stumbles forward in the dark. The mother sobs silently as she watches her dying baby. She tries to nurse it at her breast but to no avail.

The family finds another bush about a half-mile away. They move forward and attack the bush with the same ferocity as they have eight times before. This time they have luck. As the boys swing their cudgels a bump appears in the sheet. The youngest son hits it squarely and then pounces on it with both hands. "I got him!" he squeals with delight as the mother pulls away the sheet. He has a dead sparrow in his hand. Not much of a meal but better than nothing.

The family collapses in exhaustion, but nobody can sleep. The mother gives her baby to the eldest daughter and begins to prepare the supper as the father gathers fuel for the fire. The children are delighted, but the parents know that seven people cannot survive by feasting on the breast and wings of a sparrow. Nevertheless, they prepare the meal and give thanks to God. The parents eat nothing, letting the children feast as they watch the fire. A prayer of thanks is said after the meal. The mother sings a crooning lullaby as the children quickly drift off to sleep.

Morning comes and two of the boys discover a type of nut under a nearby tree. They find three of them and crack them open with a rock. The boys are starving but hand the breakfast to their mother for distribution to the family. They search for more nuts but find only the footprints of about thirty barefoot people who have cleaned out the tree some two days before.

The father guides the family southward and westward. He has a plan. They will continue moving south and west until they hit the coast. The hills and streams are barren of food, but the ocean must be teeming with life. If they can only make it before the family starts getting sick or someone dies. Fortunately, they are walking downhill. They pass several farms, but the landowners share nothing with them but water from their well. They then threaten the family with the sheriff if they do not move on.

The family finally makes it to a main road, where they find dozens of other families and many new graves. The families are all like them: destitute and poor, following the road to the ocean. There is a sickness among some, as starvation has weakened or destroyed their immune systems. The families are starving, even though several of the fields are full of wheat. Some have cattle and sheep. But no one offers them anything to eat, so the families move on.

They come upon a crowd of some eighty families who have just shared two cows and a sheep that have been donated by a wealthy landowner. It must have been quite a feast with the added "plus" of some fifteen loaves of bread. The family, though, is too late; the carcasses have been picked clean, and the farmer does not dare to share any more. He fires his gun in the air in anger as he orders the peasants to move along. He is obviously a good man, but if he gives any more, he will not be able to support his own family and hired hands. He will also not be able to pay his taxes. He would lose his property and share the plight of the poor.

The crowd moves on and comes to a crossroads where they can smell air that is thick with the aroma of boiling soup. Soup! Glorious soup! There is already a crowd of people gathered around as a Protestant minister stands before two vast iron kettles of boiling soup. He has tables laid out in preparation for a meal. There is bread and silverware plus enough food to feed a hundred families. Strangely, no one is eating at the tables.

There is a crowd milling about, but nobody is eating. The family presses forward and sees the minister standing on a stump. He has five armed men with him, plus the sheriff. The Protestant minister berates the people and tells them that they are being punished by God for their idolatry, for worshiping Mary, and following the pagan religion of Catholicism. His sermon is met with sporadic taunts and threats from the crowd, but the majority of the people are too weak to do much but listen. The minister calls for calm and offers to let them share in the feast that he has prepared if they only renounce Catholicism and mend their "evil" ways. He tells them that his congregation has taken up a collection to pay for their "salvation" by providing this glorious feast.

The crowd is silent, stomachs craving food, knees nearly giving way from exhaustion. Mothers look into the eyes of their starving children and fathers gaze sadly at their once beautiful wives. Everyone fights pounding headaches as the youngest children, tortured by the aroma of the soup, begin to cry. Someone yells, "No one goes souper!" The call echoes and reverberates through the crowd as it is picked up and repeated. An elderly lady moves forward and calls for silence. She leads the crowd as everyone kneels and prays: "St. Michael, the Archangel, lead us in battle, defend us from the malice and snares of the devil. . . ."

The prayer ends as an elderly man moves forward from the crowd and calls out: "Follow me!" He shakes a stick at the soup as he spits and moves down the road. The crowd follows. Everyone is starving, but none will deny their faith for soup. There is an exhilaration that can be felt among the crowd. They are no longer struggling but walking with a purpose as the weak are helped by those who are a bit stronger. The men carry the bigger children and the elderly. The women carry the babies. Everyone is singing religious songs.

The crowd moves across a hill and comes to another intersection where it spies a gaunt nun sitting on a limestone fence. She stands to greet the people. Although her garments cover everything but her face and hands, she has the appearance of a skeleton. Her bony cheeks and hands do not fit well under her white robes, which now appear four sizes too big. She smiles at them as she moves forward asking if they need food. The answer is obvious.

"Food is only two miles away!" she yells to the crowd as she points down a side road. The word passes through the people as they move forward. The going is difficult as everyone nears total exhaustion. The nun's white garments make her look like an angel as she leads them to a nearby village. As they journey on, the starving marchers marvel as they watch a bridge being built in a nearby field. There is no reason for the bridge as the field is flat as a table, but the men build anyway.

The crowd soon enters the churchyard of St. Patrick's Catholic Church. In the yard is a Mennonite minister stirring huge pots of soup. He offers them everything that he has. He is Welsh, but he has sold everything that he has so that he can come to the assistance of the starving poor. The nun says that he has food enough for five days.

The nun leads a prayer of thanks, and the hungry peasants form into a line. The family members grab a bowl of soup and move into the church building to sit in the pews and eat their fill. They then climb the church tower where they can look toward the coastal village below. They watch silently as tons of wheat and herds of cattle are being loaded onto ships that are bound for England. The husband and wife with the five children decide that it is time to emigrate. Ireland is no longer a good place to live now that there are no potatoes for the peasants to eat. The children are safe for a few days, but there are no guarantees for their future.

The 'Soupermen' of Ireland

Ireland was a bountiful land in the late 1840s. It was a land that was controlled by the British, who generally looked down on the native Catholic Irish. The Irish Catholics had been suppressed since the late 1500s, but persecution of Catholicism became particularly severe when Puritan and evangelical forces gained power in England in the 1600s. Men like Oliver Cromwell raised armies that conquered Ireland and massacred the Catholic populations of entire towns like

Drogheda, Wexford, and Clonmel. Penal laws against Catholicism were also passed. The Catholic Church was outlawed and many of its priests and bishops martyred.

If one were an Irish Catholic, he basically could neither own property or livestock, nor be allowed to learn to read or write. A Catholic could neither hold government office nor speak as a witness or in his own defense in court. He also had to pay a ten-percent tax to support the church of a denomination that he did not belong to. Catholics were reduced to near slavery, except that their families could not be bought or sold. If a Catholic denounced his Catholic faith he could become a full citizen and live a life other than that of a poverty-stricken peasant. Despite these pressures, few Catholics converted.

The Irish as a nation chose centuries of poverty and illiteracy rather than deny their faith. Instead the Church went underground. Catholic churches and schools were burned by the British. This did not stop the faithful who met clandestinely, holding religious services in fields, marshes, and basements of buildings.

By the early 1800s, though, many of the penal laws had been repealed, but the Irish Catholics were still poor and uneducated. The Irish land was owned by others, and few people in power cared to spend money to build the schools necessary to educate the Catholic Irish. When parents died, their Catholic children felt lucky to inherit clothes or the tools to work as renters on the farms of foreigners who owned the land.

By the time of the 1840s, when Abraham Lincoln was still a lawyer, the poor Irish Catholic peasantry was reduced to living off potatoes. The land produced plenty of cattle and wheat, but these were used to send to the high-priced markets in England and Germany. The proceeds from these sales went to pay the high rents and taxes that the landowners owed to the crown.

In about 1846 a fungus destroyed the potato crop in Ireland and much of Western Europe. The same fungus returned for several years, meaning that there was no food available that the Catholic peasants could afford. In other European countries that suffered from the potato blight, wheat and barley were made available to the peasantry. But in Ireland it was considered too expensive to waste on the poor. The poor were instead dispossessed and turned off of their rented grounds. Potatoes were not only their main source of food but one of the methods for paying rent. When the potato crop failed, the starving poor could not pay their rent and were evicted en masse.

At first they wandered the country looking for food. In 1847 ("Black '47" as it was called) the famine became particularly severe, with millions either dying or emigrating, despite the fact that food (wheat, sheep, and cattle) was plentiful enough to export to the rest of Europe.

One of the peculiar results of the famine was that the English government failed to launch an effective effort to relieve the famine in Ireland. Many English argued that the Catholic Irish were being punished for being Catholic. Others felt that this was nature's way of eliminating the surplus population in Ireland. Others called for work programs to instill a proper work ethic among the Irish. One of their programs was to allow the peasants to earn money for food by working on construction projects. There was no charity but only work farms and a type of workfare. Workhouses were established, but many of the workers were so weak that disease generally wiped them out. Others were required to work on "bridge projects." These projects were designed to require work but produce no results that might make Ireland stronger or more economically competitive. Many of the bridges were therefore built in open fields instead of crossing streams and gullies.

One of the final peculiarities of the time was that after the local Catholic Church resources were expended on charity, scores of Protestant ministers sold everything they had and went to Ireland. About half of them sold their possessions to assist the poor through magnificent acts of charity. The other half chose to tempt the Irish Catholics to convert by offering starving families "soup" if they denied their faith. This was called going "souper."

It is to the credit of generations of the Irish that they chose martyrdom or emigration over going "souper." In the Irish tradition they chose poverty, hardship, and sometimes death, rather than deny their religious beliefs and sacrifice their loyalty to the Catholic Church. ‡

The chaplain holds a crucifix
directly in front of the soldier's eyes . . .

CHAPTER SEVEN

Kyrie Eleison

~e%~

Fredericksburg, December 13, 1862

The boots of two thousand men pound the wooden planks of the pontoon bridge as the Irish Brigade, part of the Union Army, marches across the Rappahannock River. The column moves forward into the sleepy town of Fredericksburg, which lies north of Richmond, Virginia, about halfway between the state's capital and Washington, D.C. The community has been torn apart by cannon fire and then plundered by Federal troops who had been sent forward to dislodge Southern sharpshooters.

In the distance the rattle of musket fire and the constant boom of artillery can be heard. This crescendo of doom is an intense and ominous omen as to what awaits any soldier that dares to move forward toward the Confederate lines. In a nearby building a field hospital is being set up to accept the trickle of wounded soldiers that has begun flowing to the rear.

An artillery shell explodes in the air directly above the brigade. The explosion is too high to do much damage. The soldiers, though, flinch as the concussion whips the men and a blanket of wind pulls sharply across their bodies. The colonel, mounted on his white horse, raises his sword and yells, "At the double quick . . . march!" The column moves forward as a lowly private struggles to keep his canteen from banging against his thigh. With each step he takes, it bounces forward and slams back down. He puts one hand on it as he cradles his musket with the other. The column lurches forward as more shells explode in the air. Soldiers slip on muddy streets as the brigade winds its way along narrow avenues and finally spills out upon the gently sloping fields that lay on the southern edge of the town.

The regiment stops and forms up. To their front stand thousands of blue-suited soldiers, fighting unprotected in open fields as they exchange fire with the rebels on the ridge that stands four hundred yards away. The Confederate troops, however, are dug in, with infantry firing from behind a stone wall, and artillery strategically placed to gain protection from the hillside and trees.

"The generals must be crazy!" the Irish-born private thinks to himself as his regiment receives orders to drop their packs. As hundreds of men stand in formation, they let their packs drop to their rear. They do not watch where they land but look forward at the field that lies between the Union and Confederate forces. Thousands of blue-coated dead and injured litter the expanse. The field has a singularly crawling effect as hundreds of wounded try to struggle their way to the protection of the rear. The scene is a reminder of the futility of charging the entrenched rebels. "Must be some sort of mistake!" the private thinks to himself as the command "Fix bayonets!" is repeated above the din of drums, bugles, muskets, and cannons.

The clatter of bayonets being pulled from scabbards and attached to muskets punctuates everyone's thoughts. The private's stomach tightens up and adrenaline courses throughout his body. His mind is jumbled with fear. He has never been in battle, but he knows that charging these entrenched rebels will be akin to committing suicide. He looks around absentmindedly as he fumbles with his bayonet. A sergeant yells for him to hurry.

He looks at his rifle and finds that he has been pushing his bayonet ring onto the wrong part of the barrel. He corrects his mistake and the bayonet clicks into place. The flag bearer posts and soon the Irish Brigade's flag is held next to the Stars and Stripes. It is a beautiful green flag with an oversized Irish harp emblazoned across its middle. The private was told that the words *Erin Go Bragh* grace a scroll that labels the flag. "Ireland Forever," he is told, is what the phrase means. He sees the letters but cannot read. "Ireland Forever," he thinks to himself as he glances down to make sure that his musket's firing cap is in place so that he can fire at the enemy. He then cocks his rifle in preparation to fire. A possibly fatal mistake made by an untried soldier.

"Forward . . . march!" the colonel yells as he takes off his cap, places it on his sword, and waves it on high for everyone to see. The private's mind swirls with fear and emotion as the unit moves forward at a walk. Seconds pass and the brigade is ordered to trot. They are moving across muddy fields that are littered with equipment, clothing, and spent cannonballs. The brigade's flag is raised on high as the soldiers yell "Erin go bragh!" at the tops of their lungs. Their yell lets escape the pent-up tension and fear that had been welling up in their bodies. The fear and tension of men who feel certain that they are about to die.

The young private's fear returns immediately as his part of the line meets with an uneven section of ground. The irregular terrain halts their part of the column. The private is three rows back and cannot see what is delaying the men ahead of him. They are stopping and climbing a waist-high mound of earth, and the delay means that the rest of the column is moving forward at a trot while their portion of the line is stalled and bunching up.

Fear overcomes everyone as soldiers in the rear push those in the front. Those in the front lose their balance and stumble forward as they are finally freed from the barrier. The private is jostled as hands behind him push him forward into the soldier ahead of him. The private hears nothing but cursing and the distant rattle of the muskets and cannons. No one is shooting nearby. The rebels are holding their fire until they can get a better shot.

The private is finally free and trying to move forward with the rest of his formation. Horror grips his heart as he accidentally fires his weapon into the air, the bullet screaming harmlessly across the sky. His musket holds but one round, and it is gone. He rushes forward just the same, his Irish pride helping overcome his instinctive fear. The brigade finally reaches the sea of dead and wounded that litters the field in front of the Southern lines. As the private runs forward he watches the rebel artillerymen on the hill. Their leader raises his hand, then drops it swiftly, the signal for his men to pull the lanyards of their cannons. Twenty cannons spit fire and thunder as they lurch backward suddenly and momentarily stand on their tails. The private hallucinates with fear. Out of the fire springs hundreds of iron rabbits that eagerly bound and leap forward to the men of the private's brigade.

The Union soldier, his chest constricted by a sharp and sudden pain, has not been hit but is suffering the effect of an overpowering fear. The cannonballs fly and as they hit the brigade's front there is the sound like wind-driven sleet hitting a windowpane. Men scream as their bodies are torn apart and hundreds of Federal troops fall to the ground. The private's musket has been split in two and his canteen bursts, spilling water that drenches his leg. He is turned and spun by the impact of the blow but stands isolated on the field. His hands are empty and many of his comrades are gone. Some are dead, many are suffering from wounds, and others are lying unconscious or trying to find cover. Gunfire is ineffectually returned as scattered muskets spit angrily toward the stone wall.

The private runs forward to grab a wounded friend who is trying to make his way to the rear. His friend's leg is twisted and torn, a scarlet river running from his knee to his ankle. He will not make it unassisted. As the Irish Brigade soldier grabs his friend by the arm and shoulder, he notices hundreds of Confederate infantrymen popping up from behind the stone wall that lies about one hundred yards to their front. Their muskets are leveled, then a sheet of flame leaps forward. The private is lifted to his toes as he feels a sharp pain in his back and blood begins to fill his mouth. He and his injured friend tumble down like dancers twirling into the ground.

Terror consumes the private as he finds himself pinned beneath his friend. The pain rockets through his body as he lies helplessly and the battle rages around him. Men are dropping everywhere as bullets and cannonballs fly. The boom and rattle of cannon and musket fire drones on for hours, the sound punctuated by the cries of men as they call for help.

The private is certain he will die. His mind buzzes with thoughts of his wife and three children in faraway New England. Who will care for them? Who will be a father to his children? Sadness overcomes him as he mentally distances himself from the battle.

"Why is nobody helping me?" he thinks to himself. "It is too dangerous!" his mind answers as he tries to push his friend's body off of him. His unsuccessful efforts only exacerbate his despair. He looks around and cannot see anyone in blue standing, although he thinks he sees a black figure moving in the corner of his eye. "What could it be?" he wonders, trying to remember what infantry unit would be wearing black.

His question is answered by the mumbling voice that he hears only a few yards behind his head. Above the *thwack* and *zing* of passing bullets he can hear "Kyrie eleison" being whispered ("Lord, have mercy" in Greek). He listens further as the beginning of the rite of confession is being started. The rest of the rite is blotted out by the hearty yells of men as the Union Army begins another charge against the Confederate forces. The rebel artillery booms louder and their infantrymen add their fire to the clatter that lasts for another ten minutes. When the firing lets up, the private can hear a priest, a military chaplain, giving the Last Rites to several wounded soldiers. The private can see nothing, though, and waits hopefully for the priest to finish. When the sacrament has been administered, the Irish-born soldier musters all his strength and yells "Father Murphy!" at the top of his lungs. He hopes that his weakened voice will carry above the din of battle. He hopes further that the priest will find him, buried under a twisted knot of men.

The chaplain hears him and yells back: "Shaun Patrick!" He waits a minute and then bounds forward to the private. He has timed his rush carefully to occur when the Confederate muskets are being loaded. This window of opportunity lasts only a second because the rebel marksmen are not reloading their muskets but merely exchanging empty muskets with those that have been loaded by others to their rear.

The priest, however, has been successful and now kneels leaning over the young private. He is open and exposed to fire but completes his duties just the same. The chaplain is a pitiful sight. He has blood all over him. There are several bullet holes in his garments and his hat. Near misses, but reminders of the danger at hand. His left hand is bandaged, since several fingers have been shot away.

The priest, though, sadly looks down on the private and holds an eight-inch crucifix directly in front of the soldier's eyes. The private looks at the figure of Jesus and the feeling of terror begins to fade away from his heart. "Are you ready to confess your sins?" the priest asks calmly, his voice somehow penetrating the rattle of gunfire and the boom of artillery.

"Yes, Father!" the private answers with relief. The rite of confession is begun and ended. The gunfire continues as bullets fly only inches above the pair, but the private now has little fear. The priest has begun the Last Rites as he anoints the young soldier and prepares him for death. The fear and terror in the private's heart is now replaced with an inner peace. He is now ready to die. He closes his eyes and forgets his worldly cares. He rests peacefully as he prays over and over, "Kyrie eleison!" — the prayer bringing more peace than the Irish lullabies that his mother used to croon when he was a baby.

The priest bandages the wound of the private and takes a coat off of a nearby dead soldier. He places the coat over

Shaun, kisses his brow, and wipes the blood from his mouth. "I must go now to help the others," the Irish chaplain whispers in the soldier's ear. The priest disappears, but the private does not mind. "Kyrie eleison!" he keeps repeating over and over.

Hours pass and darkness comes. The battle has ended and the field is cloaked in the damp darkness and cold of a Virginia winter's evening. The private lies there, sleeping some, passing out some, and praying intermittently. He wakes to see the Northern lights, the aurora borealis, dancing like a burning snake slithering across the sky. "Rarely are the lights seen so far south," he thinks as he wonders if he is hallucinating or possibly dying. "Are these the gates to heaven?" he asks himself peacefully. His thoughts are interrupted by the return of Father Murphy. The priest is tired but undaunted.

The priest shakes the private and calls out: "Shaun Patrick!" The private wakes and smiles. His body is numb from cold as he lay under the stars. His only protection being the overcoat that the priest has provided. The chaplain produces a canteen and presses it to the private's lips. Water dribbles into the injured soldier's parched mouth. The private's bitten tongue throbs as he swallows the cool liquid. The priest pushes the bodies of the private's fallen comrades aside and moves around so that he can grab the young man by his shoulders. He pulls hard and the private is overcome by pain. The pain fades as the wounded soldier's vision goes black and his consciousness slips away. As he fades, the private is certain that he is dying, but he does not struggle, no longer experiencing the terrible fear he felt earlier. The terror is gone.

A few days later the private wakes. He is lying in a field hospital with about a hundred other wounded soldiers. To his right and left lay men from his regiment; at his feet sits Father Murphy, praying the Rosary. "Shaun Patrick," the chaplain whispers as he notes that the private has awakened. Joy overcomes the private's heart as the chaplain tells him that he is going to be okay. His wounds are severe but not life-threatening. Shaun will be going home to see his family and friends.

"We must tell your family!" the priest announces in a joyous manner. He tells the private that newspapers have already telegraphed news of the disastrous Battle of Fredericksburg. "I have already written several families to tell them how their loved ones in uniform have fared," he adds as he reaches under his cloak. The priest pulls out some writing materials and helps the private compose a letter to his family. The private talks and the priest writes. The letter is skillfully written, the priest helping the private choose "upbeat" and "loving" words to let his family know that he is all right. When the letter is done, the priest places it in an envelope and prepares it for mailing. He struggles a bit because of the missing fingers on his left hand.

When the time comes for the priest to move on, the private hugs him and thanks him for rescuing him from certain death. He also thanks him for being there to hear the confessions of his friends. The chaplain smiles and says nothing. His face then breaks into a grin and whispers to the wounded men who have gathered around, "Erin go bragh!" then turns and walks away. "Kyrie eleison!" the private answers, emphasizing his newfound motto. "Kyrie eleison," he repeats as he looks around the room at his wounded comrades. "Kyrie eleison!" — "Lord, have mercy!" These words will be with him for the rest of his life.

For those who are interested in statistics, the Battle of Fredericksburg resulted in nearly thirteen thousand Union troops being killed, wounded, or missing in action, whereas the Confederate forces suffered some five thousand casualties.

The Heroism of Military Chaplains

Throughout Christian history clerics have accompanied soldiers into battle. From the earliest times they traveled with crusaders and armies that were raised from the time of Emperor Constantine to the present. The chaplains were extremely important in that they traveled with soldiers to ensure that their spiritual needs were met, even when going into battle. Not only did the chaplains hear confessions, celebrate Mass, and deliver the Last Rites, but they also helped care for the wounded and give a Christian burial to the dead. Caring for the wounded was an important function because most armies did not have trained medical doctors or corpsmen until about the time of Abraham Lincoln.

Relatively recent history shows us that chaplains were often in the thick of battle, risking their lives to carry out their duties and care for their military flocks. In early times this exposure to combat concerned various popes. While the Church wanted its priests spiritually assisting the soldiers, it did not want the priests to take active part in the fighting. On several occasions popes issued edicts such as "forbidding priests to shed blood in battle." This confused some who told the priests that they should never carry knives or swords but could defend themselves with "maces." Maces did not "shed blood" but only "crushed bones." Luckily, few priests ever fought in battle, although many were exposed to the horrors of war.

In the Middle Ages numerous military chaplains were captured and enslaved or held for ransom. These chaplains were noted for carrying on their mission even after being captured. They continued ministering to their imprisoned comrades and often tried to convert their captors.

In the time of Cortés's conquest of Mexico we find several priests accompanying the Spanish *conquistadores*. They were exposed to many of the terrors of battle, and history shows them on several occasions hearing the confessions of men who were certain they were about to die. They also celebrated Mass and helped evangelize the Aztec peoples whom Cortés eventually conquered.

In the 1800s we also see many cases of Catholic and Protestant chaplains risking their lives to accompany soldiers on dramatic charges. The unarmed priests and ministers did not expose themselves to the fighting by participating in attacks but acted as "witnesses" to their men, showing that they were not afraid to die while carrying out their duties for Christ. The chaplains also felt a dramatic need to be with their soldier-friends to assist them spiritually during their time of need and to help them physically if they were wounded.

John Ransom, in his book *Andersonville Diary*, describes how a Catholic priest was one of the few sources of decent food and spiritual help for the inmates in the Confederacy's notorious Andersonville Prison. There are similar cases of priests ready and willing to do whatever was necessary to help others in the name of Jesus, even giving up their lives.

Take, for instance, this story of a Huron Indian preparing to be baptized in the Catholic faith. The story revolves around the brave efforts of a Jesuit priest, one who rushed bravely forward into battle to baptize an Indian friend who lay exposed and dying from an Iroquois gunshot wound. The Huron catechumen had received religious training from the priest but had not yet received the sacrament of baptism. Once wounded, he called for the priest so that he could die a Christian. The priest, defenseless, rushed to the catechumen's side and baptized him just as the Iroquois warriors let loose a volley of musket fire. The priest gave his life to complete the baptism that opened the gates of heaven for his newly dedicated convert.

In the 1900s the heroic tradition continued with Catholic and Protestant chaplains following armies and navies across the world. Chaplains serving on ships in World War II were just as much of a target as any of the sailors who manned the ships themselves. If a bomb or torpedo hit the ship or the ship sank, the chaplains would suffer the same fate as the crew.

The chaplains, however, not only served in battle but also took over many of the social support functions that kept the soldier in contact with his family. Keep in mind that, until the nineteenth century, a majority of the world's soldiers could not read or write. The chaplain, being an educated man, could often help the soldiers write letters home or read letters that they received from their loved ones.

In many cases the chaplains were indeed angels of mercy. They filled this role by alleviating the fear of the common soldier and often, by example, showing him (or her, when women were allowed to join the military) the way to a more perfect union with Christ. The chaplains regularly did this at extreme risk to their lives. Not only did they risk their lives by accompanying soldiers into battle but also by exposing themselves to disease and extreme hardship that was inherent to the battlefields of the world.

The dedication of military chaplains has largely gone unnoticed in Church history. It is likely, though, that they should be ranked high among the Church's forgotten heroes. ✝

Conclusion

I hope the preceding pages will encourage you to contemplate the lives of our unsung and forgotten Catholic heroes, to remember why they gave of themselves, giving up the comforts of life to serve others, even sacrificing their very lives.

Perhaps one or more of the stories in this little book will give you a better understanding of the preciousness of your faith, your commitment to practice it to the best of your ability, and the desire to share it with others who are seeking God. ‡

Appendix

I have included for the reader's use a summary of information that is available on a small portion of the English martyrs. The information was derived from *The Dictionary of Saints* (Doubleday, 1980) and *The New Catholic Encyclopedia* (McGraw-Hill, 1967). Please note that the legend "Oath of Supremacy" means that the person refused to take the Oath of Supremacy or comply with the Act of Supremacy, which recognized a monarch's control of the Church. The same similarly applies to other legends; for example, "Catholic priest" means that the martyr was killed for being a Catholic priest. Other legends are self-explanatory. It is also implied that before a victim was executed, he or she suffered torture and imprisonment, often for months or even years.

English Martyr	Year of Execution	Method of Execution	Crime	Monarch
John Hale	1535	Beheaded	Resisting Henry VIII	Henry VIII
John Houghton	1535	Hanged, drawn, and quartered	Oath of Supremacy	Henry VIII
H. Middlemore	1535	Hanged, drawn, and quartered	Oath of Supremacy	Henry VIII
Robert Lawrence	1535	Hanged, drawn, and quartered	Oath of Supremacy	Henry VIII
Thomas More	1535	Beheaded	Oath of Supremacy	Henry VIII
Augustine Weber	1535	Hanged, drawn, and quartered	Oath of Supremacy	Henry VIII
John Fisher	1535	Beheaded	Maintaining papal supremacy	Henry VIII
Sebastian Newgate	1535	Beheaded	Oath of Supremacy	Henry VIII
Richard Reynolds	1535	Hanged	Oath of Supremacy	Henry VIII
Augustine Webster	1535	Dragged and hanged	Oath of Supremacy	Henry VIII
John Rochester	1537	Hanged	Oath of Supremacy	Henry VIII
John Forest	1538	Dragged and burned	Resisting Henry VIII	Henry VIII
Adrian Fortesque	1539	Beheaded	Oath of Supremacy	Henry VIII
John Beche	1539	Hanged, drawn, and quartered	Speaking against Henry VIII	Henry VIII
Hugh Faringdon	1539	Hanged	Resisting Henry VIII	Henry VIII
John Stone	1539	Hanged, drawn, and quartered	Oath of Supremacy	Henry VIII
Richard Whiting	1539	Hanged	Resisting Henry VIII	Henry VIII
Richard Featherston	1540	Hanged, drawn, and quartered	Resisting Henry VIII	Henry VIII
Thomas Abel	1540	Hanged, drawn, and quartered	Oath of Supremacy	Henry VIII

Name	Year	Execution	Reason	Monarch
Edmund Brindholme	1540	Hanged	Popish Plot	Henry VIII
Edward Powell	1540	Hanged, drawn, and quartered	Oath of Supremacy	Henry VIII
Margaret Pole	1541	Beheaded	Not supporting the king	Henry VIII
David Gonson	1541	Hanged, drawn, and quartered	Oath of Supremacy	Henry VIII
John Larke	1544	Hanged, drawn, and quartered	Oath of Supremacy	Henry VIII
John Ireland	1544	Hanged, drawn, and quartered	Oath of Supremacy	Henry VIII
Jermyn Gardiner	1544	Hanged, drawn, and quartered	Oath of Supremacy	Henry VIII
Stephen Gardiner	1544	Hanged, drawn, and quartered	Oath of Supremacy	Henry VIII
Thomas Plumtree	1570	Hanged	Refused to deny Catholicism	Elizabeth I
John Storey	1571	Hanged, drawn, and quartered	Oath of Supremacy	Elizabeth I
Thomas Percy	1572	Beheaded	Refused to deny Catholicism	Elizabeth I
Thomas Woodhouse	1573	Hanged, drawn, and quartered	Oath of Supremacy	Elizabeth I
Cuthbert Mayne	1577	Hanged, drawn, and quartered	Oath of Supremacy	Elizabeth I
John Nelson	1578	Hanged, drawn, and quartered	Oath of Supremacy	Elizabeth I
John Sherwood	1578	Hanged, drawn, and quartered	Oath of Supremacy	Elizabeth I
Alexander Briant	1581	Hanged	Popish Plot	Elizabeth I
Everard Hanse	1581	Hanged, drawn, and quartered	Catholic priest	Elizabeth I
Ralph Sherwin	1581	Hanged, drawn, and quartered	Refused to deny Catholicism	Elizabeth I
Laurence Johnson	1582	Hanged, drawn, and quartered	Refused to deny Catholicism	Elizabeth I
Robert Johnson	1582	Hanged, drawn, and quartered	Catholic priest	Elizabeth I
Thomas Cottam	1582	Hanged, drawn, and quartered	Catholic priest	Elizabeth I
William Filby	1582	Hanged, drawn, and quartered	Catholic priest	Elizabeth I
Thomas Ford	1582	Hanged, drawn, and quartered	Catholic priest	Elizabeth I

Name	Year	Method	Reason	Monarch
Luke Kirby	1582	Hanged, drawn, and quartered	Catholic priest	Elizabeth I
Richard Kirkman	1582	Hanged, drawn, and quartered	Oath of Supremacy	Elizabeth I
John Shert	1582	Hanged, drawn, and quartered	Oath of Supremacy	Elizabeth I
Brian Lacey	1582	Hanged	Assisting a Catholic priest	Elizabeth I
William Lacey	1582	Hanged, drawn, and quartered	Oath of Supremacy	Elizabeth I
Richard Laurence	1582	Hanged, drawn, and quartered	Oath of Supremacy	Elizabeth I
James Thompson	1582	Hanged	Catholic priest	Elizabeth I
John Payne	1582	Hanged, drawn, and quartered	Catholic priest	Elizabeth I
William Hart	1583	Hanged, drawn, and quartered	Catholic priest	Elizabeth I
John Slade	1583	Hanged, drawn, and quartered	Oath of Supremacy	Elizabeth I
Richard Thirkeld	1583	Hanged, drawn, and quartered	Catholic priest	Elizabeth I
James Bodey	1583	Hanged	Oath of Supremacy	Elizabeth I
James Fenn	1584	Hanged, drawn, and quartered	Oath of Supremacy	Elizabeth I
Thomas Alfield	1584	Hanged	Oath of Supremacy	Elizabeth I
James Bell	1584	Hanged	Oath of Supremacy	Elizabeth I
Thomas Webley	1584	Hanged	Oath of Supremacy	Elizabeth I
John Finch	1584	Hanged	Oath of Supremacy	Elizabeth I
Richard Gwyn	1584	Hanged, drawn, and quartered	Impenitent Catholic	Elizabeth I
William Hummerford	1584	Hanged, drawn, and quartered	Catholic priest	Elizabeth I
John Nutter	1584	Hanged, drawn, and quartered	Catholic priest	Elizabeth I
Robert Andleton	1586	Hanged	Catholic priest	Elizabeth I
Margaret Clitherow	1586	Crushed to death	Assisting Catholic priests	Elizabeth I

John Finglow	1586	Hanged, drawn, and quartered	Catholic priest	Elizabeth I
Edward Stransham	1586	Hanged, drawn, and quartered	Catholic priest	Elizabeth I
Francis Ingleby	1586	Hanged	Catholic priest	Elizabeth I
John Sandys	1586	Hanged	Catholic priest	Elizabeth I
Richard Langley	1586	Hanged, drawn, and quartered	Harboring Catholic priests	Elizabeth I
William Marsden	1586	Hanged	Catholic priest	Elizabeth I
Richard Martin	1586	Hanged, drawn, and quartered	Harboring Catholic priests	Elizabeth I
Thomas Pilchard	1587	Hanged, drawn, and quartered	Catholic priest	Elizabeth I
Edmund Sykes	1587	Hanged, drawn, and quartered	Catholic priest	Elizabeth I
John Fenton	1588	Hanged	Catholic friar	Elizabeth I
Edmund Campion	1588	Hanged, drawn, and quartered	Catholic priest	Elizabeth I
Christopher Buxton	1588	Hanged, drawn, and quartered	Catholic priest	Elizabeth I
Ralph Crockett	1588	Hanged, drawn, and quartered	Catholic priest	Elizabeth I
Robert Dalby	1588	Hanged, drawn, and quartered	Catholic priest	Elizabeth I
William Dean	1588	Hanged	Catholic priest	Elizabeth I
Henry Webley	1588	Hanged	Assisting a Catholic priest	Elizabeth I
William Hartley	1588	Hanged, drawn, and quartered	Catholic priest	Elizabeth I
William Gunter	1588	Hanged	Catholic priest	Elizabeth I
Robert Wilcox	1588	Hanged, drawn, and quartered	Catholic priest	Elizabeth I
Robert Widmerpool	1588	Hanged, drawn, and quartered	Catholic priest	Elizabeth I
John Hewitt	1588	Hanged, drawn, and quartered	Catholic priest	Elizabeth I
Thomas Holford	1588	Hanged, drawn, and quartered	Catholic priest	Elizabeth I
Hugh More	1588	Hanged	Refused to deny Catholicism	Elizabeth I

John Munden	1588	Hanged, drawn, and quartered	Catholic priest	Elizabeth I
Robert Morton	1588	Hanged, drawn, and quartered	Catholic priest	Elizabeth I
Margaret Ward	1588	Hanged, drawn, and quartered	Harboring a Catholic friar	Elizabeth I
Robert Sutton	1588	Hanged	Converted to Catholicism	Elizabeth I
John Robinson	1588	Hanged, drawn, and quartered	Catholic priest	Elizabeth I
William May	1588	Hanged, drawn, and quartered	Catholic priest	Elizabeth I
Thomas Belson	1589	Hanged	Dissenting from the queen's Church	Elizabeth I
John Amias	1589	Hanged, drawn, and quartered	Catholic priest	Elizabeth I
George Nichols	1589	Hanged	Catholic priest	Elizabeth I
Richard Yaxley	1589	Hanged, drawn, and quartered	Catholic priest	Elizabeth I
Francis Dickenson	1590	Hanged, drawn, and quartered	Catholic priest	Elizabeth I
Christopher Bales	1590	Hanged and disemboweled	Catholic priest	Elizabeth I
John Edward	1590	Hanged	Catholic priest	Elizabeth I
Miles Gerard	1590	Hanged, drawn, and quartered	Catholic priest	Elizabeth I
Anthony Middleton	1590	Disemboweled while alive	Catholic priest	Elizabeth I
Polydore Plasden	1591	Hanged, drawn, and quartered	Catholic priest	Elizabeth I
Montfort Scott	1591	Hanged	Catholic priest	Elizabeth I
Ralph Milner	1591	Hanged, drawn, and quartered	Refused to deny Catholicism	Elizabeth I
John Mason	1591	Hanged, drawn, and quartered	Oath of Supremacy	Elizabeth I
Sydney Hogsden	1591	Hanged, drawn, and quartered	Oath of Supremacy	Elizabeth I
Roger Dickinson	1591	Hanged, drawn, and quartered	Oath of Supremacy	Elizabeth I
Edmund Gennings	1591	Hanged, drawn, and quartered	Catholic priest	Elizabeth I

Name	Year	Fate	Charge	Monarch
Laurence Humphrey	1591	Hanged, drawn, and quartered	Called the queen a heretic	Elizabeth I
Eustace White	1591	Hanged, drawn, and quartered	Catholic priest	Elizabeth I
William Patterson	1592	Hanged, drawn, and quartered	Catholic priest	Elizabeth I
Thomas Pormort	1592	Hanged, drawn, and quartered	Catholic priest	Elizabeth I
William Davies	1593	Hanged, drawn, and quartered	Catholic priest	Elizabeth I
James Bird	1593	Hanged, drawn, and quartered	Oath of Supremacy	Elizabeth I
Anthony Page	1593	Hanged, drawn, and quartered	Catholic priest	Elizabeth I
Edward Waterson	1593	Hanged, drawn, and quartered	Catholic priest	Elizabeth I
John Cornelius	1594	Hanged, drawn, and quartered	Catholic priest	Elizabeth I
John Ingram	1594	Hanged, drawn, and quartered	Catholic priest	Elizabeth I
John Speed	1594	Hanged	Assisting Catholic priests	Elizabeth I
George Swallowell	1594	Hanged	Converted to Catholicism	Elizabeth I
Howard Philip	1595	Died in prison	Converted to Catholicism	Elizabeth I
William Freeman	1595	Hanged, drawn, and quartered	Catholic priest	Elizabeth I
Alexander Rawlins	1595	Hanged, drawn, and quartered	Catholic priest	Elizabeth I
Thomas Southwell	1595	Hanged, drawn, and quartered	Catholic priest	Elizabeth I
Henry Walpole	1595	Hanged, drawn, and quartered	Catholic priest	Elizabeth I
William Knight	1596	Hanged, drawn, and quartered	Oath of Supremacy	Elizabeth I
Henry Abbot	1596	Hanged, drawn, and quartered	Oath of Supremacy	Elizabeth I
George Errington	1596	Hanged, drawn, and quartered	Oath of Supremacy	Elizabeth I
William Gibson	1596	Hanged, drawn, and quartered	Oath of Supremacy	Elizabeth I
Edward Fulthrup	1597	Hanged, drawn, and quartered	Catholic	Elizabeth I
William Andleby	1597	Hanged, drawn, and quartered	Oath of Supremacy	Elizabeth I

Thomas Warcop	1597	Hanged	Sheltering William Andleby	Elizabeth I
Henry Abbot	1597	Hanged, drawn, and quartered	Catholic priest	Elizabeth I
Peter Snow	1598	Hanged	Catholic priest	Elizabeth I
Christopher Robinson	1598	Hanged	Catholic priest	Elizabeth I
John Jones	1598	Hanged, drawn, and quartered	Catholic priest	Elizabeth I
Thomas Hunt	1600	Hanged, drawn, and quartered	Catholic priest	Elizabeth I
John Sprott	1600	Hanged, drawn, and quartered	Possessing a Catholic book	Elizabeth I
John Rigby	1600	Hanged, drawn, and quartered	Refused to deny Catholicism	Elizabeth I
John Pibushi	1601	Hanged, drawn, and quartered	Catholic priest	Elizabeth I
Mark Barkworth	1601	Hanged, drawn, and quartered	Oath of Supremacy	Elizabeth I
Robert Filcock	1601	Hanged, drawn, and quartered	Oath of Supremacy	Elizabeth I
Nicholas Tichborne	1601	Hanged	Catholic	Elizabeth I
Thomas Hackshot	1601	Hanged	Catholic	Elizabeth I
Anne Line	1601	Hanged	Harboring Catholic priests	Elizabeth I
James Duckett	1602	Hanged	Distributing Catholic literature	Elizabeth I
Francis Page	1602	Hanged, drawn, and quartered	Catholic priest	Elizabeth I
William Richardson	1603	Hanged, drawn, and quartered	Catholic priest	Elizabeth I
Robert Griswold	1604	Hanged	Assisting a priest	James I
John Sugar	1604	Hanged	Catholic priest	James I
Thomas Welbourn	1605	Hanged	Harboring Catholic priests	James I
Ralph Ashley	1606	Hanged	Oath of Supremacy	James I
Edward Oldcorne	1606	Hanged, drawn, and quartered	Gunpowder Plot	James I
Nicholas Owen	1606	Died of torture	Catholic priest	James I

Matthew Flanthers	1607	Hanged, drawn, and quartered	Catholic priest	James I
George Gervase	1608	Hanged	Oath of Supremacy	James I
Thomas Garnet	1608	Hanged, drawn, and quartered	Catholic priest	James I
George Napper	1610	Hanged, drawn, and quartered	Oath of Supremacy	James I
John Roberts	1610	Hanged, drawn, and quartered	Oath of Supremacy	James I
Thomas Somers	1610	Hanged, drawn, and quartered	Catholic priest	James I
John Almond	1612	Hanged, drawn, and quartered	Oath of Supremacy	James I
Richard Newport	1612	Hanged, drawn, and quartered	Catholic priest	James I
William Scott	1612	Hanged, drawn, and quartered	Catholic priest	James I
Richard Newport	1612	Hanged, drawn, and quartered	Catholic priest	James I
John Ogilvie	1615	Hanged	Oath of Supremacy	James I
John Tulis	1616	Hanged, drawn, and quartered	Catholic priest	James I
Thomas Tunstal	1616	Hanged, drawn, and quartered	Oath of Supremacy	James I
Roger Wrenno	1616	Hanged, drawn, and quartered	Converted to Catholicism	James I
Thomas Maxfield	1616	Hanged, drawn, and quartered	Oath of Allegiance	James I
Edmund Arrowsmith	1628	Hanged, drawn, and quartered	Catholic priest	Charles I
Richard Herst	1628	Hanged, drawn, and quartered	Catholic priest	Charles I
Ambrose Barlow	1641	Hanged, drawn, and quartered	Catholic priest	Charles I
William Webster	1641	Hanged, drawn, and quartered	Catholic priest	Charles I
Edmund Catherick	1642	Hanged, drawn, and quartered	Catholic priest	Charles I
Thomas Reynolds	1642	Hanged, drawn, and quartered	Catholic priest	Charles I
Alban Roe	1642	Hanged, drawn, and quartered	Catholic priest	Charles I
John Goodman	1642	Hanged, drawn, and quartered	Catholic priest	Charles I

Name	Year	Method	Reason	Monarch
Hugh Green	1642	Hanged, drawn, and quartered	Catholic priest	Charles I
Thomas Holland	1642	Hanged, drawn, and quartered	Catholic priest	Charles I
John Lockwood	1642	Hanged, drawn, and quartered	Catholic priest	Charles I
Ralph Corbington	1644	Hanged, drawn, and quartered	Catholic priest	Charles I
Henry Morse	1645	Hanged, drawn, and quartered	Catholic priest	Charles I
Philip Powell	1646	Hanged, drawn, and quartered	Benedictine monk	Charles I
Peter Wright	1651	Hanged, drawn, and quartered	Catholic priest	Oliver Cromwell
John Southworth	1654	Hanged, drawn, and quartered	Catholic priest	Oliver Cromwell
Edward Coleman	1678	Hanged, drawn, and quartered	Popish Plot	Charles II
Thomas Pickering	1679	Hanged	Popish Plot	Charles II
John Fenwick	1679	Hanged, drawn, and quartered	Popish Plot	Charles II
Nicholas Postgate	1679	Hanged, drawn, and quartered	Catholic priest	Charles II
Philip Evans	1679	Hanged	Catholic priest	Charles II
Anthony Turner	1679	Hanged, drawn, and quartered	Popish Plot	Charles II
John Wall	1679	Hanged, drawn, and quartered	Catholic monk	Charles II
Thomas Whitebread	1679	Hanged, drawn, and quartered	Popish Plot	Charles II
John Ireland	1679	Hanged	Popish Plot	Charles II
John Kemble	1679	Hanged, drawn, and quartered	Popish Plot	Charles II
William Barrow	1679	Hanged, drawn, and quartered	Popish Plot	Charles II
Richard Langhorne	1679	Hanged	Popish Plot	Charles II
John Plessington	1679	Hanged	Popish Plot	Charles II
David Lewis	1679	Hanged, drawn, and quartered	Popish Plot	Charles II
John Lloyd	1679	Hanged, drawn, and quartered	Catholic priest	Charles II

William Howard	1680	Beheaded	Popish Plot	Charles II
Thomas Thwing	1680	Hanged, drawn, and quartered	Popish Plot	Charles II
Oliver Plunkett	1681	Hanged, drawn, and quartered	Catholic bishop in Ireland	Charles II
Claude La Colombière	1682	Died in prison	Popish Plot	Charles II

About the Author

~≈~

This is Michael Genin's first publishing venture. The author and his wife, Tami, have two children: Michael and Sarah.

The author's interest in European and Church history has been the driving force behind this work. He is active in his parish, which includes membership in the Knights of Columbus, being a sponsor for RCIA, and assisting with the Boy Scout troop sponsored by the parish. In the past, he has taught a confirmation class.

Among Genin's academic accomplishments are degrees from two universities, one of them being his major in European history. He has also been awarded the honor of being a James Scholar for achieving academic excellence in his study of history. ‡

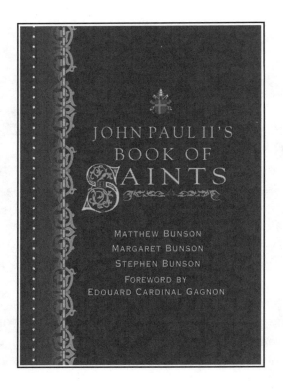

To date, the most complete list of the faithful
who have been declared saints for the entire Church.
0-87973-934-7 (934), hardcover, 368 pp.

To order from Our Sunday Visitor:
Toll free: 1-800-348-2440
E-mail: osvbooks@osv.com
Website: www.osv.com

Availability of books subject to change without notice.

Our Sunday Visitor. . .

Your Source for Discovering
the Riches of the Catholic Faith

Our Sunday Visitor has an extensive line of materials for young children, teens, and adults. Our books, Bibles, booklets, CD-ROMs, audios, and videos are available in bookstores worldwide.

To receive a FREE full-line catalog or for more information, call **Our Sunday Visitor** at **1-800-348-2440**. Or write, **Our Sunday Visitor** / 200 Noll Plaza / Huntington, IN 46750.

- -

Please send me: ___A catalog

Please send me materials on:

___Apologetics and catechetics   ___Reference works

___Prayer books   ___Heritage and the saints

___The family   ___The parish

Name_____

Address_____Apt._____

City_____State_____Zip_____

Telephone (   ) _____

A19BBABP

- -

Please send a friend: ___A catalog

Please send a friend materials on:

___Apologetics and catechetics   ___Reference works

___Prayer books   ___Heritage and the saints

___The family   ___The parish

Name_____

Address_____Apt._____

City_____State_____Zip_____

Telephone (   ) _____

A19BBABP

- -

Our Sunday Visitor
200 Noll Plaza
Huntington, IN 46750
Toll free: 1-800-348-2440
E-mail: osvbooks@osv.com
Website: www.osv.com